The CHANGE Navigator

Preparing a New Kind of Leader for an Uncharted Tomorrow

Kurt Hanks

Crisp Publications

CREDITS

Contributors: Leigh Stevens, Christy Hanks, Ilene Neilson
Illustrations: Kurt Hanks

Copyright © 1994 by Kurt Hanks
Printed in the United States of America
Experimental Edition

Single presentations and/or in-house training on this book's topic is available. Contact Phil Gerould of Crisp Publications, 1200 Hamilton Court, Menlo Park, CA 94025-9600 (800) 442-7477 for more information.

English language Crisp books are distributed worldwide. Our major international distributors include:

CANADA: Reid Publishing, Ltd., Box 69559—109 Thomas St., Oakville, Ontario Canada L6J 7R4. TEL: (416) 842-4428; FAX: (416) 842-9327

AUSTRALIA: Career Builders, P.O. Box 1051, Springwood, Brisbane, Queensland, Australia 4127. TEL: 841-1061, FAX: 841-1580

NEW ZEALAND: Career Builders, P.O. Box 571, Manurewa, Auckland, New Zealand. TEL: 266-5276, FAX: 266-4152

JAPAN: Phoenix Associates Co., Mizuho Bldg. 2-12-2, Kami Osaki, Shinagawa-Ku, Tokyo 141, Japan. TEL: 3-443-7231, FAX: 3-443-7640

Selected Crisp titles are also available in other languages. Contact International Rights Manager Suzanne Kelly at (415) 323-6100 for more information.

Library of Congress Catalog Card Number 93-70920
Hanks, Kurt
The Change Navigator—Preparing A New Kind Of Leader For An Uncharted Tomorrow
ISBN 1-56052-211-9

The
CHANGE
Navigator

Preparing a New Kind of Leader for an Uncharted Tomorrow

Contents

"Toto, I have a feeling we're not in Kansas anymore."

Dorothy, in the *Wizard of OZ*

Navigating the Unexpected

INTRODUCTION

If you, like most people, believe that the future will be just a continuation of the past and that conventional thinking will solve tomorrows problems, business-as-usual with more-of-the-same, this book is probably not for you.

On-the-other-hand, if you are one of those adventuresome few who believe we are headed into a stormy future of extreme change, that we are rapidly sailing into undiscovered waters and can't navigate them using the conventional viewpoints and old maps of the past, this book may be of help.

I wish I could talk to you in person instead of between the pages of this book. We could just go for a walk and talk to each other, exchanging ideas and experiences about how change has affected and is affecting our lives. We could then work together on getting a handle on how to respond to these changes before things get even more turbulent.

I've been dealing with this issue of change and how to more effectively handle it for over 15 years. With the dramatic changes in my life the last few years, it has become an even more pressing issue for me. If your life echoes the same, we may need to talk, and it will have to be through this book. This is the second best approach, but it will have to do.

This book is built on the idea that the key to handling change is in our thinking, specifi-cally in our perception. How we discern what is happening determines our response, and the results of our response will determine whether or not we survive and thrive in a world driven by dramatic change. Here are some stories to illustrate what I'm talking about.

The Few Who Saw That They Needed To Get Out

In October 1944, when he was 10 years old, Mihaly Czikszentmihalyi (now a psychologist at the University of Chicago), his mother and the rest of his family took the very last train out of Budapest just before the city was bombed to smithereens. He recalls, "What amazed me was that all our relatives denied the obvious. They kept thinking that everything would turn out for the best. Within a few months they all died, either from starvation or from the bombing."[1]

Throughout Europe, before WW II, and during its progression, there were stories just like this one. These stories were about people who saw things differently than the majority around them, and got out safely before it was too late. The disquieting fact is how few.

Blinded or Seeing Opportunity

In 1947, the transistor was invented by Bell Laboratories, the research arm of AT&T. Almost immediately, it became obvious that the transistor would replace the bulkier, more expensive and less reliable vacuum tubes, the key components in any radio or television set.

But nobody did anything about it—at least not in America. The leading American manufacturers were proud of their Super Heterodyne radio sets, which were the ultimate in craftsmanship and quality. These manufacturers announced that, while they were looking at eventually using the transistor, it would not be "ready" until "sometime around 1970." In their opinion, there was no hurry.

Sony was practically unknown outside of Japan at that time, and it was not even involved in consumer electronics. But Sony President, Akio Morita, saw the potential of the transistor and quietly bought a license from Bell Laboratories to use the transistor. He paid the ridiculous sum of $25,000. Within two years, Sony produced the first portable transistor radio, an inexpensive model that weighed only one-fifth as much as a comparable vacuum tube radio. With prices that were only one-third that of a vacuum tube radio, Sony captured the entire United States market for inexpensive radios by the early 1950s, and within five years, the Japanese had captured the world market as well.[2]

In 1492, Christopher Columbus, the Italian navigator, sailed west to claim new lands and trade for Spain. He was obsessed with the idea that you could sail west to China and the Indies.

At that time sailors knew that the earth wasn't flat; they just believed that the distance was too great to sail west to reach the riches of the East. They thought that a ship would run out of fresh water and food before it would ever reach landfall. So voyages to trade with India and China hugged the coast and traveled land routes.

But Columbus believed you could make it to the East by sailing west, and after seven years of talking, finally convinced Isabella to bankroll his venture.

Nobody had traveled west before this time, but word spread throughout Europe about Columbus' discovery, and it wasn't long before many ships under various flags were sailing west.

Columbus insisted that he had found the East Indies. He even called the inhabitants Indians. He wanted the rewards and exclusivity that came with this discovery, but he lost his royal financial support. His original agreement was violated in 1495, when others were authorized to sail west. Staying with this obsession, he pressed his claims in court until his pauper death in 1506.

Unthreatened View from the Top

Some Japanese automobile companies, seeing a way to expand their market with increased profits, moved into selling the higher-priced automobiles. They could make more money selling an expensive car than selling an inexpensive one.

In recent years, a former executive who worked for Mercedes Benz told me about their internal reaction to the introduction by the Japanese of their higher-end models such as the Infinity, Acura and Lexus into the American market to compete with Mercedes.

At the U.S. Mercedes Benz headquarters, he heared refrains such as "The Japanese won't compete with us—they can't." And, "We don't need to do anything to meet their competition," and, "We have a superior product."

The executive felt differently, and left the company. With a dramaticly sliding market share as Japanese competition slashes into American sales, quite different statements are heard today at the headquarters.

Seeing Only One Way Out

A friend's wife, overloaded with increasing pressures of life and a large family, progessively exhibited strange behavior. She would eat only cabbage or only string beans, or one other food obsession, and nothing else for months. As expected, her health rapidly deteriorated, and she found herself being force-fed in the hospital.

As her conditioned increasingly worsened, she was taken to specialist after specialist until she found herself being examined by the top doctor in his field. He made a very interesting statement: "I can't help her, nor can anyone else. She is a very intelligent woman, more than the doctors who see her. And she has made a decision to die. Until she sees things differently and changes her mind, there is nothing I can do."

This woman had made a decision. She saw her situation as impossible, and having been raised in a very strict religious culture, she created the only way out. She concluded she must die in a socially acceptable way by making herself sick and then dying of the illness.

The last time I heard, she was in a nursing home, still trying to die and still being force-fed.

The Same Underlying Pattern

What do all these stories have in common? Each story is from a very different setting, yet all have the same underlying pattern:

People are making choices based on what they *see* will get them what they want. All these stories are about human perception or people's mindsets in a world of change. Part of a family realized they had to get out of a war zone, while all the others didn't. Columbus saw a way to the riches of the East, but failed to perceive that he had discovered even more. Some companies recognized and seized opportunities; other companies didn't. And finally, one member of a family, observing the increasing pressures affecting them all, decided to opt out, while the rest viewed things differently and continued on.

The theme reverberating throughout all of these stories, which is connected to you and I today, is: Our collective and individual future will involve dramatic and unexpected change. How we view or see things will determine our reactions to that future. Those reactions will determine if we thrive, or even survive, in this coming new world.

Increasingly, all of us face this world of *Exponential Change*. Change so rapid and unexpected that we can't react in any effective way with conventional approaches. What we see as 2+2 will not always equal 4 anymore. Our traditional perception of what is really happening will increasingly fail us. We need to fundamentally modify how we respond to these unexpected instabilities.

In these previous stories, the people were able to react based only on how each one saw his or her world. They could respond in no other way. Our discernment determines our response, and our discernment is determined by our mindsets or paradigms.

For years, I have been working on a process to help people to modify their mindsets to respond differently and much more effectively to this *Exponential Change*. It is a method to empower a person in navigating the stormy waters of the future, to become a ***Change Navigator.***

Since this book involves change, you wouldn't expect it to be done in a conventional manner, would you? So, the following pages are designed as a transition into the book's unique format and approach.

Introducing Some New Concepts and Terminology

In this book, I'm using some words in new ways and creating some totally new terms. Using these new words and working with metaphors was the only way I could conceptualize and communicate, what on earth, I was talking about in this mindset-changing process. The people and situations I worked with were often so varied that, only by teaching a new terminology around a central metaphor, could we work together.

So now, in order for you and I to work together, I'll provide some definitions of the main terms and concepts used in this book:

Alignment: How well people's mindset maps match the actual or real territory they find themselves in.

Atlas: A collection of mindset maps about something in particular, such as how to make yourself rich, relating to the opposite sex, standing in line at a store, or wiggling out of things that people ask you to do.

Change Navigator: One who, in a world of accelerating change, helps individuals and organizations become more adaptive by increasing their discernment. Change navigators do this by reading other's maps, showing them where their maps will lead them and then providing alternative maps. They can also do this even more effectively by teaching the entire mapping process.

*What a **Change Navigator** looks like, and the proper attire for formal navigating.*

Collusion: A relationship in which each person provides the other proof of the correctness of his or her individual mindset map. They often subliminally support one another into camouflaging the underlying falsity of their mindsets in order to avoid the fear and pain of accepting things as they really are.

Concept Maps: Graphic summaries or visual interpretations of concepts to be communicated. This book is infested with them.

Denial: Lying to oneself and others about the conflict one is having between ones map and the actual territory. Trying to hide a questionable or invalid map behind an idealized map, making others believe one is following the ideal.

Discernment: Seeing things as they really are. Not getting caught in how things should be, ought to be, hope to be, or fear the most, but how they actually are. Then, using this insight in making effective and responsive choices.

Growth: The constant refinement and updating of what is on your maps.

Guiding Concept: A verbal or written interpretation or summation of a particular mindset map.

Invested Map: Mindset maps that have a lot of ego, time, money, hope, pride, rationalization, etc., invested in them to the point where a person can't change them without losing something he or she considers very critical. This investment is often more important than any lack of truth found within the map.

Map Box: A mental map, as with a regular map, is a representation of the real territory of actual experience. But once made, a mindset map naturally creates a world of its own that reflects the constraints and descriptions drawn on the map. This world is a self-contained box separate from the real world, and it surrounds and supports the map inside it. This box can make people blind to seeing beyond their map's defining limitations.

Map-Lock: A determination not to change your mindset map no matter how much evidence indicates that your map is in error.

Mapping: The mental process of creating mindset maps. We create these maps by interpreting the patterns of our own experience; we borrow them from others, our culture, television, etc.; and we possess a few maps that are inherent to us.

Mindset Map: A mental construction interpreting how the real world works. It is used as a guide for how we choose to respond or navigate through

This is an actual **Mindset Map** *of a well known public official, made visible through the miracle of modern mapping techniques.*

life's many situations. These mental maps define us and our interactions, and give us a sense of place and purpose. They guide all our relationships with people, nature, ideas—everything.

A *Mindset Map* is a schema, a prototype, a mental model or a paradigm of the way things are. In fact, the word paradigm is from the Greek word paradigma, which means a pattern or map for understanding and explaining certain aspects of reality. A *Mindset Map* is like the playing board of a board game. We follow it to play out moves and interact with others in various situations to reach some end. It is like a scale model home we have inside us, representing the real home we live in. We have thousands of maps we follow every day, such as the map of how to stand in line at the supermarket, or the map of how to treat your boss when he gets upset, or even the map of what you are now doing.

Navigate: To steer a course using a mental and/or real map along a route heading towards a destination. The sequence of interactions with another, dictated by what is found upon reading another's mindset map. Its purpose may be either to get something you desire or to move him or her toward some particular point where he or she becomes more adaptable to change.

Non-invested Map: Mindset maps that have little or nothing invested in them to stay the same and that could easily be modified or replaced if a better map comes along.

Pain Quotient: How much conflict someone or a group can take between what their mindset map says a situation should be like and what it actually is, before they will accept making a map shift. His map says, "He must like the children's cat because he needs to show them he loves and accepts what they have," but the actuality is that

the animal keeps destroying the house and furniture. How much damage will it take before the cat is removed and the map changed to another description of what it is worth to gain the children's approval? This is the pain quotient.

Remapping: The process of correcting or replacing an old map with a new one. It is the process of making mind shifts (or map shifts) and is usually done because an old mindset map doesn't work.

Responsiveness: Adapting to rapid changes in a particular situation with speed and a sense of appropriateness, and with a goal to achieve the optimum desired results that are possible.

Stewardship: The responsibility a navigator has to help a person(s) adapt to rapid change. These persons may be family, friends, coworkers, employees, etc. . .

Supporting Evidence: Gathering proof to support a particular mindset map. "It is windy so we must be in Chicago," "She didn't ask me to the party so you see again that nobody likes me," and "I've received a nomination to be on the board of directors by clear headed people who recognize my great leadership abilities."

Terrain or Territory: Reality, truth, things as they really are. Let's not catch ourselves chasing our tail here in rhetorical and philosophical questions about "what is truth?" or "what is reality?" Truth is just a process of continual approximation.

Unresolveable Bind: Having conflicting mindset maps in one moment, demanding choice. This can be a very painful situation, emotionally and otherwise. One map says, "You're an honest person," while the other map says, "You need the money owed them much more than they do." Both maps demand a response—now! Neither map will work. Within the situation there is no solution.

I don't expect all these definitions to make complete sense now, but they do familiarize you with the terms and concepts within this book.

What follows next is a series of concept maps (a new term) explaining the unique format of this change navigator training manual.

Visual Bias

The way we have gained knowledge was gained in the past is most often the expected and preferred mode for gaining knowledge in the future. **People prefer any new information in the mode they have received and accepted it in the past.** Since the audience for this book has been saturated in visual data for years, this book is also very visual. Also, the subject matter in this book deals with seeing relationships, and the very essence of visual language is dealing with relationships. In other words, the language fits the content.

The dominant mode of learning in the past generation was the spoken or written word.

The dominant mode of learning in the present and in the future is the visual image.

The first generation of TV watchers is 37-47 years old.

The next generation of TV watchers is in their late twenties to mid-thirties.

The following generations of TV watchers and video game players are now entering the workforce.

. . . and so on!

Why Put It into Pictures

People are biased. We like things the way they have been. And we don't like it when someone tries to force another way down our throats. But that is exactly what many leaders, instructors, trainers and teachers are doing today. They are forcing many of us to digest mountains of information in ways that most of us no longer want. We are biased toward a more visual approach.

Past generations were biased to the written and spoken word. People gained information from books, newspapers, radio and speeches. In work and school, people were taught through lectures and books. Information was transmitted almost solely through the written word. Anything visual was only an appendage to the word.

Then along came TV. Children raised on TV are now over 40 years old, working (many in leadership positions) and raising families. Take a look at this profile of the first TV generation:

- They are the baby boomers.
- Their old radios and radio programs were junked almost overnight with the advent of TV.
- They get most of their news from the TV instead of the newspaper. And even the newspaper is taking on a more visual magazine-like appearance.
- They like data and facts put into graphics—computer business graphics.
- They are moving into middle management—positions of power.
- They spend much of their free time watching TV.
- They prefer other sources of information to be like TV: bite-sized pieces, visual, quick, etc.
- The early television shows such as Milton Berle and Pinky Lee changed how we handle information.

All these generations have a strong bias toward visual presentation of information. In a survey, over 90% preferred visual over verbal and written material. This is one of the main reasons this book was put into such a visual format. Here are the key points in how this book and process is presented:

- All content is structured first and primarily visually and symbolically.
- Whole frameworks or maps of the material are presented first, and then various routes through these maps are taken.
- Information is packaged into short, easily discerned segments so you can access the information as needed and desired.
- Visual and written cues are used to tag the important information for future finding and remembering.
- Visual metaphors and stories are given to illustrate all key concepts.
- Material is presented in tight, independent units.

"By the middle of the next century, some analysts say, even our language will be transformed. Letters and words will gradually give way to a new system of communication based on visual images."
U. S. News & World Report

Through actual teaching situations in schools, from elementary to college and business training, it has been proven repeatedly that visually presented material is better remembered and utilized than verbal or written material. With these points in mind, and the fact that the entire process of mindset mapping is mainly a visual process anyway, it is the way this book had to be done.

Why does this book have such a different format? When both sides receive information in a more receptive form, the entire brain assimilates information more effectively. **The format of this book matches as much as possible the way the brain naturally functions.**

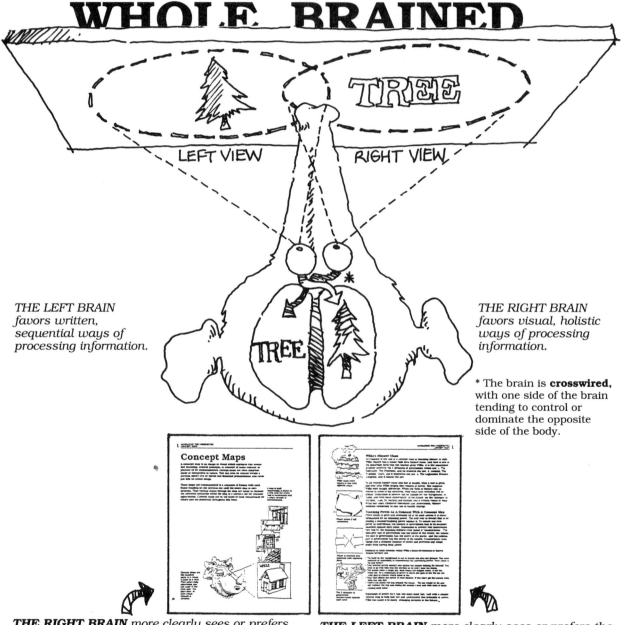

WHOLE-BRAINED

LEFT VIEW   RIGHT VIEW

THE LEFT BRAIN favors written, sequential ways of processing information.

THE RIGHT BRAIN favors visual, holistic ways of processing information.

* The brain is **crosswired,** with one side of the brain tending to control or dominate the opposite side of the body.

THE RIGHT BRAIN *more clearly sees or prefers the left field of vision. To more effectively communicate, visual and holistic information should dominate the* **left page or field of view.**

THE LEFT BRAIN *more clearly sees or prefers the right field of vision. To more effectively communicate, written and sequential information should dominate the* **right page or field of view.**

Utilizing the Whole Brain

The human brain has two halves, each one preferring a different way of processing information. The left brain, which is primarily connected to the right eye, favors the verbal, written and sequential ways of communicating. The right brain, which is primarily connected to the left eye, favors the holistic and visual way of communicating. That is why people who are right-brain dominant tend to sit on the right side of classrooms and theaters (so they can fill their left field of vision) and left-brain dominant people tend to sit on the left side of classrooms and theaters (so they can fill their right field of vision).

Most publications and educational materials are produced by left-brain dominant people. Therefore, those publications have a left-brain bias. But the approach presented in this book is unique and it does take some time getting used to.

Because of this proven concept, I matched the format in this book to the preferred ways of brain processing for better assimilation and retention of the contents of this book. The visual and holistic information is put on the left (it is also put first), and the written and sequential information tends to be on the right.

This book is presented in a format to match the way the brain processes information.

This format is used because remembering and recalling key concepts and ideas is critical to the success of you using the information in this book. It is of little or no use if you can't recall or utilize what is communicated within these pages. Using this brain processing format, you will probably find that retention and understanding, and consequently, application, will increase dramatically.

As the Book Progresses

However, this book progresses from communicating information that is basically conceptual and defining in its nature at the beginning into teaching knowledge that centers on the understanding of process towards the end. I've found that teaching "process" knowledge can be better accomplished if the reader imagines situations where the concepts are being applied. Stories can involve the reader in this mapping process more than visual images on a page. Images in your mind's eye often can be far better than any you can actually see with your real eyes. These stories can involve parts of the brain in much the same way that the visual format is an attempt to do. So, as the book progresses, the format of the book will change. I'm still dealing with whole-brained thinking; it just won't be as obvious as in the beginning.

Concept Maps

A concept map is an image or visual which captures the essential meaning, central principle or concept of some subject or process to be communicated. Concept maps are often diagrammatic or metaphoric in nature. They can even be created within a person's mind's eye by stories and theatrical presentations and never be put into an actual image.

These maps are communicated in a sequence of frames, with each frame building on the previous one until the entire map is constructed. Then, I take various routes through the map to connect the concepts contained within the map to a person's life for possible applications. Concept maps can be self-made or built sequentially by others and are presented throughout this book.

A map is built sequentially, a frame at a time, until the entire map is constructed and a whole concept is communicated.

Concept Maps are like building parts of a house a piece at a time. Then when fully assembled, you can walk in the front door, or the back door, or even crawl through a window.

20

Willie could learn history in two very different ways.

Power grows if left unchecked.

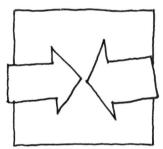

Power is checked and balanced with opposing force.

The 3 divisions of government counterpoised against each other.

Willie's History Class

The following is an example of the use of a concept map to teach history to kids:

Willie Makett has a junior high-level history class. One of the important facts that the teacher gives Willie is the separation of power between the three divisions of government, which are: 1. The Executive Branch, The President, and he enforces the law; 2. The Judical Branch, The Supreme Court, and they interpret the law; 3. The Legislative Branch, The Congress, and they enact the law.

This fact is taught in the typical history class. Then a test is given, and over time, Willie forgets this concept of power. But suppose Willie were taught differently. If the facts of history were related to some of his concerns, both value and retention would increase. The separation of powers concept can be applied on the playground, at home and, even more importantly, in Willie's future as he prepares for the changes he will face. Also, by putting this concept into a central visual or map, Willie can more effectively remember and understand. History, then, becomes something he can use to handle change.

Power tends to grow and overcome all in its path unless it is counterbalanced by an opposing power. The only way to thwart this is by putting a counterweighing power against it. To ensure our own power as individuals, the centers of government had to be counterbalanced against each other. Separation of powers was understood very well by the founding fathers--they called it "counterpoise." The executive part of government has the power of the sword, the legislative part of government has the power of the purse, and the judicial part of government has the power of life tenure. Counterpoise puts things into a dynamic balance of power and prevents any single entity from having total power.

Examples in other contexts within Willie's frame-of-reference:

• The bully in the playground is out to pound him into the ground. He needs someone or something to counterpoise the bully's increasing power. Willie's sister is big and mean.
• His brother serves dessert and makes the largest helping for himself. Willie needs to go with his brother into the kitchen so he won't take too much.
• Two people share a single pie; each wants the biggest piece, if not the whole pie. So a separation of power is made: one gets to cut the pie, the other gets to choose which piece is his.
• Willie's Dad offsets the power of his mother. If he can't get the money from mom, he asks Dad.

With these examples, separation of power isn't just one more dead fact. And with a simple concept map to help him see and understand this principle of power, Willie can apply it to many different situations in his future.[15]

A Subconscious Process Made Conscious

Mindset mapping is bringing a natural mental process that is largely done unconsciously, up into awareness. When we become aware of process, we can see it clearly, work with, play with it or change and modify it in specific desirable ways. Then this modified natural mapping process can be released to return to unawareness to carry out future modification automatically.

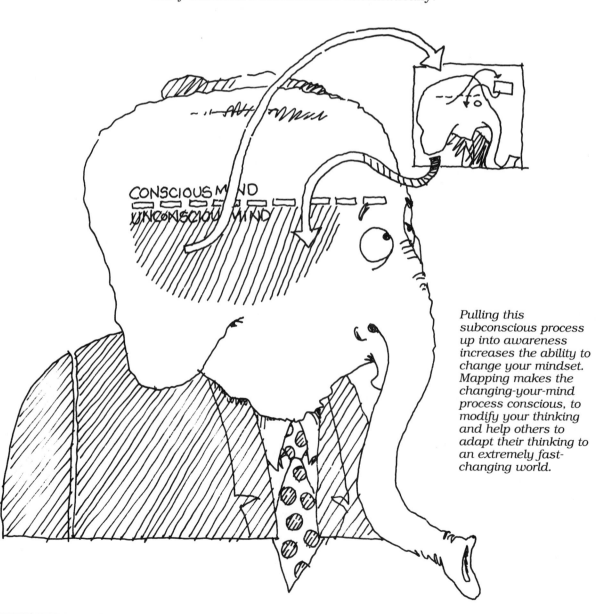

Pulling this subconscious process up into awareness increases the ability to change your mindset. Mapping makes the changing-your-mind process conscious, to modify your thinking and help others to adapt their thinking to an extremely fast-changing world.

Bringing A Hidden Process Into View

The process behind Mindset Mapping is not something new, unique or special, but is the ordinary activity of thinking. A problem arises because usually it is subconscious or below the level of awareness. It is like breathing we usually are not aware it is going on. We seldom think about our thinking and assume it is beyond our discernment and any need of improvement. So, we seldom change our thinking and our responses to situations, but continue in the same old mental rut.

If we make this natural process more conscious, we can become more aware of how mental mapping works and alter it to better suit our needs. Using this process with awareness helps us to adapt to an accelerating rate of change. The mapping process is made conscious, and we can more clearly see our maps to modify or correct them to better fit our needed responses. *Mindset Mapping* makes our thinking, and thus our behavior, more understandable, controllable and applicable. And, like consciously working on your backhand in tennis, you get better at doing it.

By deliberately and repeatedly working through the stages of *Mindset Mapping*, the mind soon adapts to the process. It becomes natural to shift your thinking into another realm of *"thinking about your thinking"* and what is going on as all of us respond to various old or unique situations. You can gain control over something that you thought was beyond deliberate control by seeing the connections between map, choice, situation and response.

Making this mental process conscious is like my neighbor teaching his daughter to ride her bike. He worked on separate items such as coasting, parking and watching for traffic. Then these items are fused together into the natural and automatic process of riding a bike. Her dad made this process conscious at first; then she worked at it. It became so natural, she didn't have to think about it at all. She just rode her bike. Now, she is making the process conscious again as she learns to modify the process of bike riding with a motor scooter she is learning to drive. Then this, too, will become unconscious and automatic.

Often heard statement: "This process is nothing new. I have always done it this way. *Mindset Mapping* just makes it obvious and puts everything together, so I do what I've always done, better."

1. Your mind naturally creates and follows the mental maps you make, but you are usually unaware of it and have no control over these maps.

2. Mindset Mapping lets you see this mental mapping process by making it conscious.

3. When this process is again made unconscious, your thinking power is markedly improved to handle change.

A Parable:

The baby was raised to adulthood only on a Monopoly playing board. All she knew how to do was related solely to playing the game.

Once there was a little baby who was raised to adulthood on a giant Monopoly game board. All this baby ever knew was Monopoly: how the playing board is laid out, how to follow the rules, and the ways to win the game. Her entire world was defined by the edge of the board. It was all she knew, all she had ever known. She knew the playing pieces, the community chest cards, the little red hotels and where Boardwalk was. She knew to pass "Go" without going to jail while collecting $200, how to accumulate the best properties and to line up all the money for easy identification of the different denominations. In short, life was the game, and the game was life. Her name was Sally.

Playing the game of Monopoly was simply the only thing there was. It was superior to anything else, because there was nothing else. It was life itself. Sally learned that the game defined everything, and by understanding more of the game, she could understand everything in life. The rules were logical, rational and objective. The purpose was to win, to keep the game going and to be competent at the game, even to become a master.

The game must be played with others, and all interactions between people were dominated and colored by the game.

You can't play monopoly alone; others are needed in the game. As Sally grew up, she found others to play the game with her. Sometimes winning, often losing. Over the years, a very large box had grown up around all the players, encasing them all within its bounds. And there within the box, the now grown baby and all the other players used up their time in life playing the game of Monopoly.

Then something happened. Sally slowly began to feel that something was wrong. Deep down inside, very deep inside, next to her heart, something unnameable felt off, out of place and not quite right. When she mentioned this to the other players, she was told, "You're crazy. You just need to try harder and win more." The other players, attempting to comfort Sally, made the statement, "Winning is the purpose of life." If she could just win more often, with more effort on her part, then things would be better and she would feel better." With these words she was given a little extra help with an additional throw of the dice and a few more bills to play with.

Still the feeling persisted, and Sally began to wonder again, "Wasn't there more to life than Monopoly?" She often thought it was she. She was wrong, maybe even crazy. But the feeling wouldn't go away even as she played the game with increased fervor. And then there were the nights, those blasted nights! When the feelings came in the strongest. She was physically hurting, especially in the chest. It was like someone was standing on her chest. Something had to be done.

The little red hotels were losing their importance in her life.

Then one day she decided she wanted out. Why that day and at that time, she didn't know; but she wanted out. But out to where? Wasn't this all there was? Wasn't life playing Monopoly? She began to ask for help, but help from whom? Her fellow players thought she was just going through a phase and would be back playing the game with increased earnestness anytime. All the game players seemed blind to her feelings. Everyone seemed to grow progressively more compulsive, more obsessive and especially more dangerous to her and her opposing feelings. The players who won often and had more invested in the rewards of Monopoly tried harder and harder to stop her and her feelings. She also seemed more and more powerless to control or change the game into anything that would rid her of or even calm these feelings down. Then even her very existence threatened the game, and other players attacked her. Sally was feeling numb.

The outsiders, hearing the call for help, started pulling her out of the game. She, fearing for her life, started to scream.

Unknown to her, there were other persons outside the game watching her and hearing her cries for help. To them, the game was crazy, insane or odd and they wanted to answer her cries for help. So they simply walked over to the large box, reached through and grabbed her by the arm and began to pull her out. She, feeling their pull, became scared and feared for her life. After all, she was being pulled out of all she had ever known and all she had ever lived. As the pulling from the hands coming into her world from the outside increased, panic turned into terror. She was going to die. She bit hard into one of the hands that was dragging her from the game. "Atlantic Avenue would no longer be available to her. And the red hotels! What else was there?" she moaned. But the outsiders knew she needed outside help, had asked for it, and that she was powerless to leave without their help.

As the pulls and tugs increased, she oscillated inside and then outside the box, feeling she was dying, but never doing so. She feared the chaos of the unknown. Seeing this, her game-playing friends rushed to her aid, and a tug of war developed between the inside players and the outsiders, with Sally screaming for life and limb. Finally, the outsiders gave a mighty tug and out she flew.

There she was outside the game and looking in. She wasn't dead. In fact, she was very much alive, more so than she had ever been before! Where before, her world was definable, knowable and seemingly safe, from her new vantage point, she found it was only an imaginary box in a much larger universe of mystery and power. Sally no longer suffered the pain she had felt inside, where all she knew was the game, playing God with everything defined and known, but feeling powerless. She found herself loving the new magnitude and mystery of where her new home was, with a kind of power and awareness she had never known before.

From the outside it could be clearly seen that the entire Monopoly game was about to end.

From this new vantage point, she could see that the Monopoly game was about to end. Looming threateningly over the box containing her former colleagues and friends was a huge hammer, poised and ready to come crashing down on the box, game players and all. The game was almost over.

Seeing that her former colleagues would be hurt, she went into the box to warn them. She, having an outsiders view, tried to warn those on the inside. trying to relate now, as well as she could, to those friends on the inside. They looked at her sudden appearance in shock, and upon listening to her warnings, called her, "crazy and evil!" They proceeded to attack her. First verbally, with the fearful yelling, and finally, physically, throwing her out of their world, out of the box. "Why don't you see that you have choices? Why can't you see it is time to get out of the game before it is too late?" She warned them to no avail as she was thrown into what was, to them, hopelessness and nothingness.

Now, standing on the outside of the game, she saw the inevitability of what was about to happen to her former friends. Sally kept whispering to herself the following question, "How do you warn the insiders, who only see the game and nothing else, that they are about to suffer some very dramatic changes?"

A Different Kind of Leader

The Few Leaders Who Prepare Their People for an Unpredictable Tomorrow

PROBLEM: Too many of today's leaders are dealing with a rapidly changing and drastically different world by using the concepts and methods of the past.

For decades, even centuries, the stereotype of the leader has been one of a dynamic, "in charge" type of person (typically a male), standing at the top of his organization—issuing orders, making decisions and allocating the resources under his command to accomplish his objectives. The organization was often just an extension of this single person at the head giving commands.

There may be a better way to lead, one more attuned to today's organizations and their challenges.

This stereotype seems to have its roots in earlier centuries when the strong leaders were kings or military commanders, and later, industrial czars who ruled by fiat and wielded almost life-and-death powers. Even today, managerial leadership often consists of a leader who is a monarch, lord of his domain.

27

A Stable Environment

Everyone is familiar with the historically based leadership structure that has long functioned in many of our organizations— the strong decision maker at the top of the company, the division or the department, supported by a pyramidal structure placed under the executive. This is the leading typical organization:

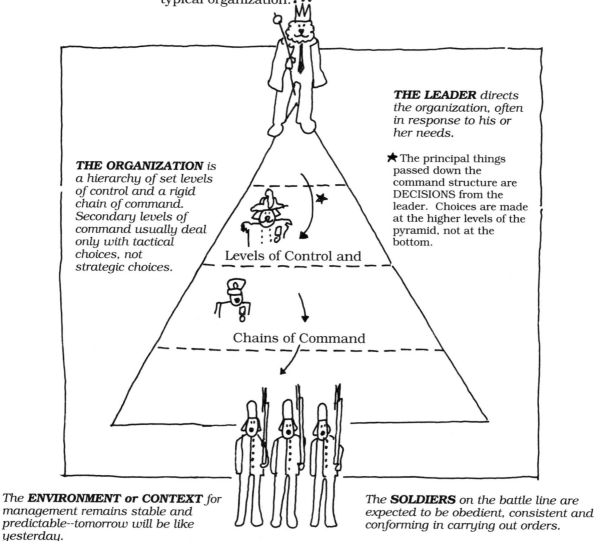

THE LEADER directs the organization, often in response to his or her needs.

★ The principal things passed down the command structure are DECISIONS from the leader. Choices are made at the higher levels of the pyramid, not at the bottom.

THE ORGANIZATION is a hierarchy of set levels of control and a rigid chain of command. Secondary levels of command usually deal only with tactical choices, not strategic choices.

Levels of Control and

Chains of Command

The *ENVIRONMENT or CONTEXT* for management remains stable and predictable--tomorrow will be like yesterday.

The *SOLDIERS* on the battle line are expected to be obedient, consistent and conforming in carrying out orders.

The role of this kind of organization is to follow the decisions of the leader. Everyone is expected to follow commands, procedures and tradition. Deviation from expectations is punished, and diversity is undesirable.

The "Leader as Monarch" or "The Authoritarian Leader" concept describes many kinds of organizations—not just kingdoms or armies or businesses, but also unions, government agencies, even families. In fact, to many people, this model is the only way an organization is structured; any other organizational model is seen as weak, chaotic or ineffective.

In a STABLE working environment, the rigid pyramidal organizational structure can survive and often thrive, with its high degree of centralized control and clearly established lines of authority and communication.

To this point in history, the pyramidal organization has often been highly successful. Some examples:

The typical organization is pyramidal, with a commanding leader at the apex, passing decisions down to conforming and obedient troops at the bottom.

- The authoritarian family provided economic security and social continuity, and established set role models for each succeeding generation. The father was the monarch, handing down edicts and decisions to the wife, who acted as the husband's lieutenant in implementing the decisions with the family.

- In the 19th century, the institutions of British government ruled a worldwide empire where all officials knew their place and carried out the wishes of the crown as passed down a rigid chain of command.

- Ford Motor Company became the preeminent American automobile manufacturer in the first decades of this century through a rigid pyramidal organization with the autocratic Henry Ford at its apex.

- In World War II, the pyramidal structure was effectively used to marshal the economic and human resources of democracy to achieve victory over formidable opponents. While the world political situation at that time was highly unstable, the American political environment was stable, united by the Axis threat.

This type of organization works well in a stable, predictable environment.

- The Catholic church has existed world-wide for centuries with a set organizational structure, with an autocratic leadership running from the Pope and Cardinals, all the way down to the local village priest.

- A family-run chain of clothing stores has operated successfully for years. The grandfather was founder of the company and still runs the company with a fair but iron hand. Generations of family have depended on him and the stores for their livelihood.

Chained by Past Successes

But there's a weakness in the traditional pyramidal organization. Its very success in the past creates a tendency to think that the successful strategies of the past will also work in the challenges and opportunities of the future. But what if that future is vastly different from anything previously faced?

Just because this way of leadership was effective in the past doesn't mean it will be effective in a fluid and unstable tomorrow, one very different from anything ever seen or experienced before.

An Unstable Environment

In the past, tomorrow was predictable—change occurred slowly, with time for adjustments and course corrections when needed. But now we are in the midst of a period of accelerating change, with events and trends coming at us so rapidly that our understanding of them often is obsolete even before we have grasped their meaning. How does the typical pyramidal organization fare when tomorrow is different and increasingly changing and unpredictable?

THE LEADER *will become fearful because he isn't getting the response he expected. He tightens the screws, increases control, stresses tradition, and proliferates new rules and regulations to deal with the changes.*

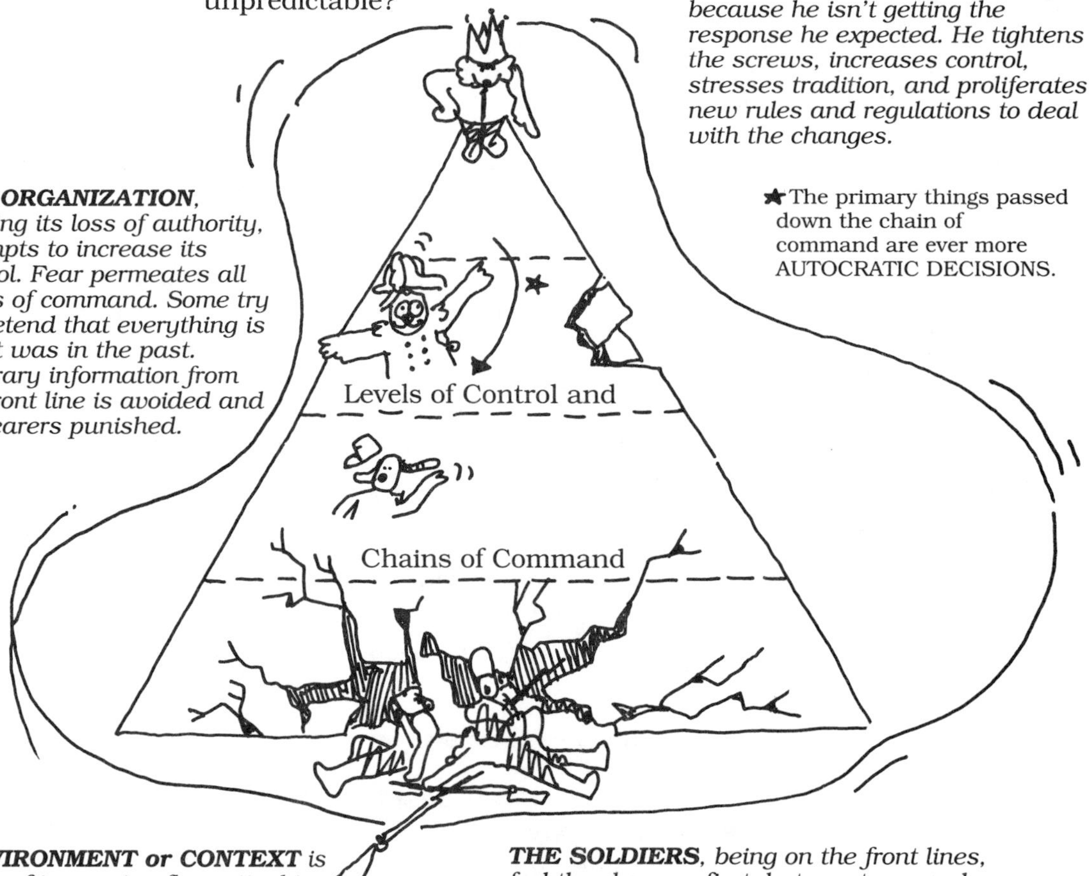

★ The primary things passed down the chain of command are ever more AUTOCRATIC DECISIONS.

THE ORGANIZATION, *sensing its loss of authority, attempts to increase its control. Fear permeates all levels of command. Some try to pretend that everything is like it was in the past. Contrary information from the front line is avoided and its bearers punished.*

Levels of Control and

Chains of Command

THE ENVIRONMENT or CONTEXT is *in a state of increasing flux, attacking the status quo.*

THE SOLDIERS, *being on the front lines, feel the changes first, but must respond according to the rules and suffer accordingly.*

Scared by change, the lack of predictability and the lack of the usual responses, the "Monarch" leader tries desperately to preserve the status quo. He may increase the emphasis on rules and conformity, or he may develop a facade of seeming to change, becoming a "benevolent king," for example, but the old mindset remains.

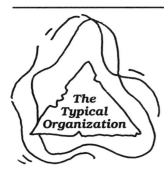

The Typical Organization

In an unstable environment, the one-time assets of centralized control may become liabilities that can destroy or damage the organization.

In an unstable environment—economically, politically or socially—a leader will not be able to get a high degree of control in the organization unless he or she possesses extraordinary charisma and people skills. In the more usual situation, increasing central control in a turbulent environment causes inflexibility and hastens collapse. Change can accelerate to a speed beyond the ability of the organization's structure to adapt in any of its existing forms and with any of its existing approaches.

In an UNSTABLE environment the organization that dogmatically follows set rules, procedures and centralized leadership control may be setting itself up for confusion, conflict and probably disaster. Here are some examples:

• Generals have historically prepared to fight the previous war. In 1939 Poland's horse-mounted cavalry was crushed by the blitzkrieg of Hitler's Panzer tanks. During the early days of the Civil War, advancing lines of foot soldiers, the standard battle tactic during the low-muzzle power era of flintlock muskets, were literally slaughtered by the new high-powered rifles. In these and other cases, the old order of battle didn't work in the more dangerous new contexts.

• The traditional American education system, with rigid administrative hierarchies and equally rigid classroom organization, curriculum and instructional methods, is based on educational ideas that originated more than 300 years ago in Germany. In the gradually evolving society of the past, this system and its refinements have provided ever-larger numbers of students with a superior education. But today, faced with accelerating social and vocational changes, the old system is beginning to falter. Achievement test scores fall, facts taught in some disciplines are obsolete before students graduate from college, parents wonder why their kids aren't learning, and taxpayers increasingly resist footing the bill. And the educators maintain that all that is needed is better pay and a return to "the basics"—a strategy of entrench and demand.

• The family-run chain of stores can't keep up with the changing demand in styles and price. The grandfather refuses to give up control of the firm to younger management. He insists he has made it successful up to this point and will continue to do so in the future. After all, "We've faced worse times than these," and, "We can't fire or move anyone. They are family!"

Responds As Expected

The monarch leader under siege can be expected to respond with the approaches that worked in the past. When they don't work, fear and avoidance dominate the organization. In extreme cases, such as Hitler's Germany, the leader functioning as a monarch may even destroy the kingdom rather than step down or change his position. An unstable environment causes fear, and fear typically increases the exaggeration of the usual controls over the organization. The same controls the autocratic leadership had used to direct the organization in the past are taken to absurd extremes. This increased control thwarts the ability of the system to adapt. This failure to adapt then makes the environment more unstable, and so on, accelerating a downward spiral into total collapse.

The Adaptive Leader

There's another kind of leader, one still concerned with the performance of his or her people and the accomplishment of the goals of the organization. But this kind of leader is a teacher, a counselor, a coach, seeking to empower people to take control of their individual work contexts. The goal of this kind of leader is to make subordinates at least as competent as he or she is. Rather than seeing subordinates as potential rivals, this leader sees them as colleagues.

THE ORGANIZATION *values performance over form, with long-term performance valued over short-term. It can adapt to changing environments. There are fewer levels of command, more networking and informal links between people. Trust between all the players is critical.*

THE LEADER *empowers others with basic principles and concepts they must understand in order to make correct decisions on their own. Overall organizational performance and adaptability are an obsession. The leader sees diversity in opinion as a strength.*

The principal leadership activity is **teaching,** *with the goal of* **empowering,** *testing and fitting employees for performance and adaptability. The most important thing taught is how to make decisions, and the most important decisions are about the changing future.*

THE ENVIRONMENT *we can expect in the foreseeable future is one of constant flux, with both dangers and opportunities.*

EMPLOYEES *feel that they are* **colleages,** *not subordinates.*

This leadership approach contains a seeming dichotomy—the best way to maintain control in an unstable environment is to give it away. And control can be delegated in such a situation only if the subordinate's competence approaches or exceeds that of the delegator. There just isn't time in an unstable situation to go back up the chain of command for tactical decisions.

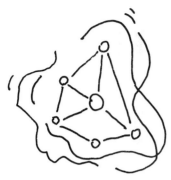

An unstable environment appears to be inevitable for all, and in a changing context, the adaptive organization, with a leader as an empowering teacher, can adapt and grow.

How the two kinds of leaders view the same employee.

An organization is like all other living things in times of stress and change, it must adapt to its new environment or die. The more rapid the change: the more adaptable the organization or organism must be in order to survive.

In an UNSTABLE environment, the leader who best empowers his or her people to adapt to dramatic changes increases the chances of survival. So led, the organization may even thrive. Perhaps the most critical skill for all persons in the organization is the ability to make correct decisions, especially in the dynamic future we face. This involves being able to read the patterns in a situation, identify the principles or processes at work, and make the choices that will advance the organization's and the individual's interests and objectives. The ultimate objective would be to have all persons in the organization capable of making correct decisions in any situation for which they have responsibility. Some examples:

- With Syrian MIGs less than five minutes from cities in Israel, an Israeli fighter pilot is trained to make decisions regarding enemy intentions and has command authority to initiate appropriate responses.

- John Wooden, the legendary coach at UCLA who won more NCAA basketball championships than anyone else, was distinctly unlike most coaches during a game. Rather than shouting and trying to command his team from the sidelines, he was always a picture of almost detached calm. The secret? Wooden drilled his players in the basic principles of the game and taught them to make their own decisions on the floor. When the game was on, he largely left the playing of the game to them, with impressive results.

- Tom Peters, in his book *Passion for Excellence*, says, "Coaching is face-to-face leadership that pulls together people with diverse backgrounds, talents, experiences and interests, and encourages them to step up to responsibility and continued achievements, and treats them as full-scale partners and contributors."

- A successful political campaign leader reported the secret of his success in this way: "We moved quickly to form our team and made sure that our team members were familiar with the larger campaign strategy, not just their particular job. With training and trust, we were off and running at a time when our opponents were still thinking about what to do."

- With autocratic leaders (leaders as a monarchs) these factors are typically present: rules, form and predictability dominate the organization, an over emphasis on facts, their ego is at stake on decisions, they look to the past and tradition for answers, and they are rigid and unmovable in their position. But with adaptive leaders, these factors are often present: emphasis on results and adaptation dominate the organization, principles and ideas have equal status with the facts, their ego can be put on the shelf, they look to learning from the future as well as lessons from the past, and they are adapting and movable in their position.

Today's leader must empower his or her people to make and carry out decisions to adapt to rapidly changing situations. The stakes are high, often including the very survival of the organization itself.

The Change Navigator

The *Change Navigator* is the role that is most critical for the adaptive leader during times of extreme and dramatic change for the adaptive leader. Helping others and yourself through these challenging and trying times can be rewarding, both in terms of survival and in the chance for tremendous opportunities. In the past, when discoverers traveled into unknown seas, the navigator had the role of getting them there alive and with what they needed to expand the opportunities open to them at their destination.

The adaptive leader sees subordinates as colleagues, not potential rivals.

The key is to empower, the goal is to change, the role is to navigate change, and the purpose is survival.

A Future of Exponential Change Is Here and Now

Since all organizations—military, social, religious or business—are inevitably marching into the same unstable future, we may in the end have no choice. As Abraham Lincoln said at the outset of the Civil War, "The dogmas of the past are inadequate for the stormy present and future. As our circumstances are new, we must think anew, and act anew."

Survival and finding opportunities were the key purpose of the navigators in the past and still are today.

If institutions are faced with adapting or dying, it is imperative that new leadership strategies be found that make adaptability possible. Much of the present focus on excellence is aimed at identifying what the currently successful companies are doing in an increasingly challenging business environment. Making the shift in thinking from *The Autocratic Leader* to *The Adaptive Leader* appears to be an important part of the kind of new strategic thinking that is needed.

At present, the few leaders who are helping their people adapt to change are conspicuous by their contrast with the norm. Perhaps in the near future, such leaders will be in the majority. Increasing the number and influence of such leaders may be the critical factor in the future of our businesses, government and other institutions as well as in our own individual futures.

The Most Important Question

One critical need is helping yourself and your people deal with change. They need to be able to adapt and handle the quantum change as it pushes in from all directions on them. Conventional material seems inadequate for what is needed. In fact, the things taught may make your people even less able to deal with the future. So, the question surfaces, what is worth giving others for the rapidly changing and unpredictable world of tomorrow? But again, even if leaders admit that for survival in the future they must assume the role of helping their people adapt to change, then the question again arises: how do I empower them to adapt to change?

Becoming a Change Navigator

The process within this book has to do with helping people handle change. The process is a decision making tool that an adaptive and empowering leader can use to help his stewardship deal with changing their discernment and thereby changing their reactions and increasing their responsiveness to change. With this process the adaptive leader becomes a *Change Navigator* leading him or herself and others through the stormy waters of change. **The role that is most crucial for adaptive leaders and for the survival of their organizations, during times of exponential change, is that of a** *Change Navigator.*

The Fall-Behind Point

The natural state for an individual or group is to stay in balance with their setting or environment. But with an ever accelerating rate of change in the situation, the responses to restore that balance aren't fast enough; they are forever playing catch-up. A **Fall-Behind Point** has been reached where they can't adapt and restore balance with this exponential change.

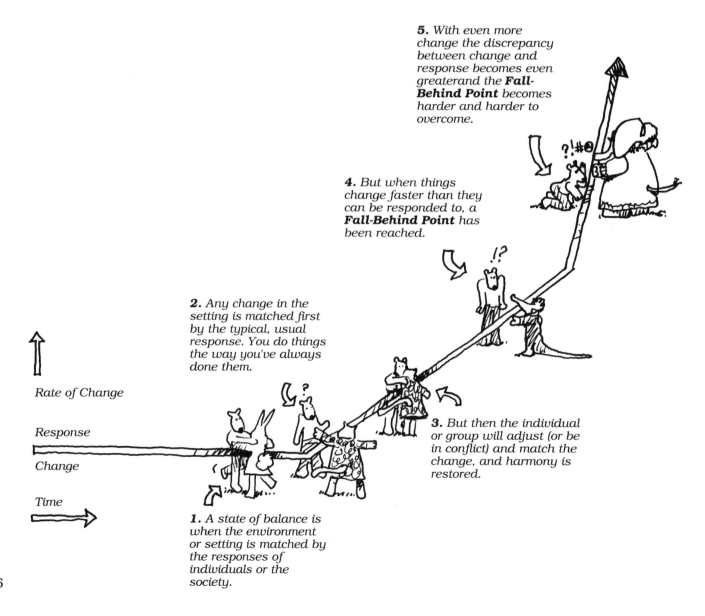

5. *With even more change the discrepancy between change and response becomes even greaterand the **Fall-Behind Point** becomes harder and harder to overcome.*

4. *But when things change faster than they can be responded to, a **Fall-Behind Point** has been reached.*

2. *Any change in the setting is matched first by the typical, usual response. You do things the way you've always done them.*

Rate of Change

Response

Change

Time

3. *But then the individual or group will adjust (or be in conflict) and match the change, and harmony is restored.*

1. *A state of balance is when the environment or setting is matched by the responses of individuals or the society.*

36

In Rhythm with the Situation

The individual's or group's desired state is one of balance or harmony with their situation or environment. If a change occurs, people will respond until balance is achieved with their first responses, these being the successful ones of the past.

- The first automobiles were buggies without the horses. They still had the buggy whip holder mounted on the side.
- When Wayne was hired by another company, he modeled his activities after the successful company he had left.
- When little Johnny entered kindergarten, he expected the teacher to be like his mother.

When things change, past responses don't work. A continual oscillation between the change and the various responses happens until, given enough time, the situation is finally met with an appropriate response and everything again regains its equilibrium.

- As time continued, the automobile became its own unique adaptation to changing technology; Wayne had trouble at first with his new company, but now he has even been promoted; and Johnny has adjusted to kindergarten.
- The early southern European explorers spread Catholicism, which was first resisted by the captured nations, but later assimilated into their society by the insertion of many beliefs and rituals that they originally had into Catholicism.
- After World War II, Japanese warlords and their equivalent rebuilt their kingdoms into corporate enterprises, channeling territorial expansion into international corporate growth.

A Sometimes Fatal Dance

With ever increasing change, the responses aren't fast enough. Things reach the **Fall-Behind Point where changes in response can't catch up to the rate of changes in the situation. Around this point is where the *Change Navigator* is most needed.**

- The Incas fought the Spanish invaders under Pizzaro as they had fought the other Indian tribes they conquered. Their empire collapsed.
- The American car companies treated the foreign car companies in the 60s as no competition whatever and continued their market battles with the other domestic car companies. They later lost a large share of their market to foreign companies.
- The arrival of Boyd's new baby was treated like they had their first child, but that experience was not with a handicapped child.
- "First it was alcohol, then pills, then cocaine, then crack, and now one designer drug after another. How do I deal with it all?" replied the police officer.
- "With two deaths in the family and the financial difficulties, she just sat there staring out the window."
- "The old answers wouldn't work anymore," said a laid-off manager.

We are always in a dance with the context we find ourselves in, trying to match our rhythm to the movement of the environment and have the environment move to us.

*One paramount problem is that people have a rough time knowing when they have reached the **Fall-Behind Point**. They become so involved in finding predetermined solutions that they become blind to outside alternatives.*

37

Discernment

An unstable environment is the need, responsive people are the goal, adaptive leadership is the vehicle, change navigator is the role, this book contains the process, and discernment is the solution. Change is only adapted to by changing. Only by changing ourselves can we hope to deal with the changes in our society. But **since we respond only to what and how we see things ,we must see anew**: looking behind the facades where most people stop, seeing deeper than most people look, viewing our situations with new eyes; then basing our responses to the incredible changes we face on the newfound insight.

Are you the few who really see, or are you the many who think they do?

Most people never really see what is going on. They just stare at their preconceived notions and previous reactions. Fearing most the clarity of the situation, they view only through the fears and dreams of how things ought to be rather than how they really are. Thereby, they lose the power that is always contained within the truth.

Discernment: *The art of seeing things as they really are. The ability to see what is actually going on, not what you are supposed to see, want to see, or fear seeing.*

". . . the first lesson of evolution is that the inability to adapt in a turbulent environment is fatal."
Stewart Brand

What is the most critical thing done by the *Change Navigator* during these turbulent times when the fall-behind point is reached? What does the navigator do when people can't react fast and effectively enough to extreme changes in their world? These stories illustrate the answer:

• In the 70s in central Africa an epidemic started in a small village. The disease was so virulent that it killed almost everyone in the small village. When a local medical team moved into the area to help, they too were caught by the disease. They rapidly became ill, and all ended up dead in a matter of days. After that, a European medical unit of doctors and nurses was sent in to deal with the disease. Most of them also died before they found out what they were dealing with. Everyone sent into the village was dead in a very short time.

Finally, someone responded with the most effective approach possible—they did nothing. They quarantined off the entire area. Where the diseases they were used to could take months or even years to run their course, even in most deadly strains, this disease didn't. This unknown diseased killed its host in a matter of hours. It seemed the disease was so deadly and spread so fast that the most effective response was to stop feeding it. The disease, once contained, acted like fire deprived of fuel—it simply burned itself out. Someone saw this weakness of the disease. It killed its hosts too quickly and died with them before it could spread between people when all human contact was stopped or slowed.

• When Chrysler motors faced bankruptcy and the company was up against the wall for its very survival, seeing clearly was the most important thing the people involved could do. Under Lee Iaccoa they saw a new market in a new product—the minivan. This product, along with some blunt talk and the vision of the realities facing the company, enabled Chrysler to regain its momentum.

• An urban myth with a point about discernment: A semi trailer got caught under a bridge. It was an old bridge built years before vehicles needing a much higher clearance appeared on the scene. As the vehicle was wedged under the bridge and the traffic built up on either side, a crowd of onlookers gathered. Each person in turn offered a possible solution to the dilemma. "Cut into the bridge," said one. "Link a wrecker to it and yank it out," urged another. "Just leave it there as a warning," laughed a third. Then a little boy strolled up to the accident scene and offered the obvious solution, "Let the air out of the tires."

• When the explorer Magellan appeared in the harbor at Tierra Del Fuego (at the bottom of South America), the local Indians didn't even see the ships. Their view of the world couldn't comprehend such a thing as a sailing ship, and their mind refused to let them see the obvious. It took the religious leaders, the shamans, to tell them the ships had arrived and anchored in the harbor.

All these stories have to do with discernment, the art of seeing things as they really are, especially when those things are new. **What is**

39

needed during these times of accelerating change, so fast it reaches the fall-behind point, is for the navigator to teach people to really see. Discernment increases the effectiveness of any response and also increases the ability to read the approaching change before it arrives and it becomes too late to adequately adapt.

It is surprising that discernment isn't really taught. The scientific method, with its need for objective observation, is the closest thing to it. But the scientific method is often stopped cold as soon as it gets to human feelings, and the problem is that most people's adaptations to change are determined by their feelings. Besides, as I've experienced, teaching discernment is an art much more than a science. It has subtleties and nuances, with its center being more often in the heart than in the head.

The trouble with our times is that the future is not what it used to be.

Paul Valery

Also, our institutions and social organizations, like the family, seem built on the need for the reverse, to not really see. Their very continuation is often based on the ability to not see the obvious. I can remember coming out of a particular meeting and thinking I must have gone completely crazy. Everything the people said and did in the meeting felt insane. It was at a large university, and key individuals were deciding on who the next chairman of a department would be. After some discussion it was admitted that it had to be a particular man. "He has all the qualifications, the degrees," said one person. Then another piped up, "He has tenure." Finally all agreed he was the one to be chairman, but with one voice they unanimously concluded, "He is absolutely incompetent." I could go on for the entire book with similar stories. But this institutional and individual insanity, with its denial and pretending, will have to end if we are to react to things as they really are. We are in trouble unless seeing the truth as it actually is becomes a critical need.

Discernment makes a person more responsive to the dynamics of change. Perception is the key to change. If you see differently, you react differently and you adapt.

"Where there is no vision the people perish."

Proverbs 29:18

Mindset Maps

How We Create Mindset Maps to Understand How the World Works

Mindset Map: A conceptual tool to discern and predict individual and group behavior in a changing environment.

Out in front of every person is a large map through which he or she sees the world. It is invisible to all but the trained eye. Each map is a representation of the world and how it works to its owner. It is a map of the territory the owners find themselves in: where they are, how they got there and how to get where they want to go. And written on each map (by its owner) is a series of explanations, guides or principles which direct the owner's behavior. It is called a mindset map. Through it we see the world. It is a naturally occurring phenomenon for all humans. Everyone, from your nephew to the President of the United States, has an individually drawn map hanging out in front of him. His life is consistent with what he has written and mapped on this thin sheet of often transparent paper.

We all create a mindset map explaining our world, our position in it and how it works.

We have created with this map a mental model of our world. This map serves as a guide in our decision making. It lets us know where we are and our possible future directions. We judge everything we come in contact with through our own mindset map. We do this because we believe that everything written on and mapped out on our individual map is true.

The better you can see what is written on an individual's mindset map, the more you can predict future responses, explain past actions and motivate needed changes. When you can discern what is written on a person's mindset map, you are more able to understand the reasons for his or her behavior.

41

The Mindset Map

We all have *Mindset Maps* through which we view the world. Everything we do, how we react and what we see is modified and directed by these maps. It is an individual creation we often accept as unquestionably true. They are our windows on the world that often create a world of their own. Always faulty to some degree, our *Mindset Maps* are forever destined to be an approximation of outer reality.

These individual's maps are an interpretation of how their world is supposed to work. These maps are constructed on every facet of their life and they will guide all choices as they travel throughout the territories the various maps apply to. They are their mindsets about all relationships to ideas, people, institutions, things, etc. These maps are the guides to follow throughout their lives.

I DESERVE **SPECIAL** CONSIDERATION

All information coming in and any choices going out are governed by their mindset maps. What they see or don't see is governed by their maps.

If you have some interaction with this person, read her mindset map in the situation and you will see how best to respond.

These guiding maps are like a belief window through which all incoming information and outgoing reactions must pass. The window through which we view and interact with the outside world.

Mindset Maps are often invisible or hard to see, but they are a common characteristic of us all.

Dogma: *Believing your map is the only one and is absolutely true and others must have it too.*

How the Discovery Was Made

It came during a time when I was working with a millionaire. I had worked with him on an occasional basis for years. Over all this time he had exhibited a lot of very strange behavior. In the early years, before he had made his money, we thought he was weird, but when he became rich, he was just eccentric. With a laugh and a shrug, people he worked with would explain his sometimes-strange behavior as a result of sunspot activity or tight shorts.

Then, while attending a meeting with this man, I saw the reason for his strange behavior. It was a meeting where I didn't have to do anything but be there; my body needed to fill a chair, but my mind could be on Mars. As the meeting progressed, I suddenly had a flash of insight. I could see his mindset map—just like it was sticking out in front of his face.

And I could also see one of the principles written on the map: *MY way is the RIGHT way, and I see things absolutely correctly.*

The invisible had suddenly become visible. I could see the future and the disasters that would be mine if I continued to work with him. I could also see the past and the thread that tied those years of erratic behavior together into a coherent pattern.

Put yourself in my shoes and you can see the power of understanding that single principle on that person's mindset map: If a person who has bought that principle were to join you in a business venture and the business failed, whose fault would he feel it to have been—his or yours? In a disagreement over management marketing directions (or anything), who would have the only correct view? As long as that idea was written on his map, could you ever possibly come out on top?

Having that insight was a life-saver for me economically. After realizing that the patterns of his behavior were all consistent with that principle, I broke off my business association with this man. Later, I warned others who were involved with this person. Several said: "Don't get all worked up. Things are going to work out just fine. You've got to be crazy not to go in with us."

Half a year later the words were, "How I wish I had listened to you. I thought you were nuts, but I was the one who was crazy. It's one thing to lose a good deal of money if you're wealthy like him, but it is another if you are not."

Since that time when I first discovered the mindset map, I've seen them around just about everyone. Being aware of other people's maps (and my own) has proven to be an essential tool in all of my dealings with others.

43

The Mindset Map

Some more thoughts on mindset maps. Mindset maps are often invisible or hard to see, but they are a common characteristic of us all. Everyone has a series of individually drawn or constructed maps.

• *These maps define what we do or don't do and what we see or don't see.*

• *Our individual needs provide the power, and the principles written on our own maps direct that power.*

• *We are constantly scanning our environment using the maps for specific satisfactions to our needs.*

• *The things written on the maps include our prejudices.*

• *Our expectations are also written on our maps.*

• *We cannot behave inconsistently with our own maps. Our own maps control our decisions.*

• *We create maps to satisfy the basic human need to make order out of the chaos of existence.*

• *We create these maps to standardize how we deal with the world. Having to deal with each event or situation in life as if it is unique and for the first time would overload our ability to function.*

• *The maps created may be true or false, they may work or not work, or any degree in between.*

MOTHER IS ALWAYS RIGHT AND TAKES TOP PRIORITY

• *Maps are made up of the materials the mind has, such as impressions, words, images, kinesthetic feelings, etc. For example, we may have a touch map of the keyboard of a typewriter. When asked to recall the position of the letters, we can't do it, but we can still sit down at the keyboard and type away.*

• *We create our maps from experience. We borrow some maps from others like our parents, family and friends. We have even collected a few maps from watching television.*

• *Our beliefs on how things work are on the maps*

• *We often consider what is written on our maps to be absolutely true, with no possible alternative.*

• *We often spend more time looking at and following our maps than we ever spend looking at the real territory. We think they are one and the same.*

• *The biggest change in your mindset maps can be the fact that first you have them, and secondly that they are in continuous need of correction and updating.*

People have many maps on all aspects of their lives, but these maps are all directed by just a few maps that direct the following of all the others.

The contrast between the two tries at singing was dramatic. The only difference was the material drawn on the man's mindset map.

The Mindset Map Defines Our Limits and Sets Our Capabilities

The three stories given here illustrate how our windows define our behavior and influence how we make decisions and relate to other people:

• A few years ago, I was astonished by what I saw at one of those traveling hypnotist shows. One particular little man volunteered to be hypnotized, and was first asked to sing. His voice was raspy, and he hesitantly got through the song even with the laughter of the crowd.

He was put under by the hypnotist and quietly told he was a world-famous singer about to give one of his finest performances. He was before a huge audience who had paid over $20 each just to hear him. He was then asked to sing again. The difference was dramatic. This time, he was quite good and very pleasing to hear, not twenty dollars worth, but still a great deal better than anticipated.

• My friend Robert has a need to be valued by others and seen as a person of substance and means. He drives a BMW, wears British suits and Italian shoes, and just got back from a European vacation with his Swedish wife.

Robert's consistent behavior allows us to read some of the governing principles on his mindset map. One of them seems to be: *My value as a person is shown by the quality of the possessions I own.* Another map is: *European culture and products are of the highest quality.*

• John learned love from a family where love was given unconditionally and freely. No matter what he did, his parents still loved him. His father once said, "Even if you killed someone, we would still love you, even on the electric chair."

Mary learned love from a family where love was given conditionally. These words, even if never said out loud, were always present in family relationships: "We love you if you do what we want, but we don't love you if you go against what we feel is best for you."

John and Mary got together, fell in love and were married. They often told each other the words, "I love you." The loving words were identical, but was their meaning? Did their individual maps define the word love the same? Would they follow their emotional interactions on their maps the same way?

Using Maps Is the Way We All Travel Through Life

Map making and map following is the way we all create order and meaning in each of our lives. It seems to be the way our minds and perceptions are naturally wired. But becoming aware of this natural ability and gaining conscious control over our map making can make enormous changes in our lives and the lives of others, especially in a world of rapid change. We can adapt more quickly by changing our maps to match the changes in the environment rather that follow the slow natural process of subconsciously remaking our maps.

The words were the same, but was the meaning?

Map Learning

Mindset maps are creations in our own minds that we make to explain and deal with the complexity of reality. **We create these maps through our interpretation of the underlying reason or meaning of experience. We do this over time through multiple frames of recurring experiences. We also borrow or get many of our maps from others: our parents, teachers, friends, leaders, television, etc.**

Here is an explanation of how we obtain our maps by taking others, maps and by interpreting and explaining the common pattern in similar experiences:

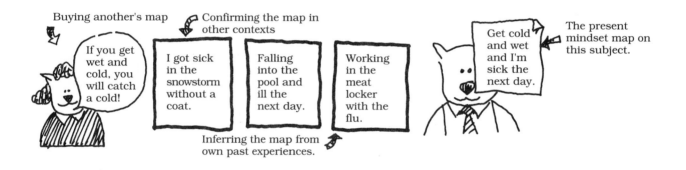

Buying another's map

Confirming the map in other contexts

If you get wet and cold, you will catch a cold!

I got sick in the snowstorm without a coat.

Falling into the pool and ill the next day.

Working in the meat locker with the flu.

Inferring the map from own past experiences.

Get cold and wet and I'm sick the next day.

The present mindset map on this subject.

Past   **Present**

I GET MY MAPS FROM THE NEWS MEDIA

Interpreting the experiences and inferring the consistencies of the past, then putting them into a map to follow.

Another person may acquire from others, maps and interpret the same experiences entirely differently, even in the same family.

Buying and Creating Maps of Our World

The mind is a map-making machine. Making maps and using them is a natural process that everybody does. It is automatic. We are creating, confirming, buying and updating maps every day of our lives. Each of us has thousands of these maps on every area of our existence to guide us through life.

Many of our maps we buy from others: from our mother and father, from our cousins, from our third grade teacher, from our friends, from television, etc. I got an interesting map from my first grade teacher: It is a song about the alphabet. If you look very close at my lips, you can see me still sing under my breath the stupid song to find things in alphabetical order.

We also construct some of our maps from our own experiences. We do this by interpreting the patterns of our past experiences. Here is another example of a map I got as a kid. I call it the little black dog map. Repeatedly as a little kid I was bitten by little black dogs. Not big dogs like shepherds or collies, which I had for my own dogs, but only little black dogs; no other color, just black. One bite was so severe I spent some time with doctors and still have scars in these battles for life and limb. So I carry around this map about little black dogs. The nasty little creatures always bite. And any time I'm around them, I end up kicking them and they end up trying to bite me. So I have proof the map is absolutely true. (Of course these two map examples are childish and childlike. I confess them to show you how we collect these mindset maps through life, and I bet you've got a few like these too.)

Maps are created to explain and deal with reality. We create them through our interpretation of the underlying reason or meaning of experience. We do this over time through multiple frames of experience. They are explanations of how life works and how on earth we can get through it. They are the road maps for survival.

A mindset map, even if borrowed from another, will be treated as your own and become such a part of you, you will often forget where you got it and even consciously that you have it.

A mindset map is like watching and remembering a movie. It is akin to the holistic impressions we have of a movie after we view it a frame, a sequence and a scene at a time. Once a movie is watched, you then have a whole map or model of the movie in your head. And with this model or map of the movie, you can relive, recall and interconnect any part of the movie in any order you want. For example, the older movie Star Wars (which most people have seen) was built frame by frame and scene by scene until you have a whole map of this movie in your mind. Then you can wander through it in various ways, not just in the sequence you received it in, and you can utilize various parts of the movie any way you like, remembering first the final award ceremony, then the cantina scene, meeting Ob1, and finally saying, "May the force be with you."

47

Map Futuring

We use mindset maps to predict the future. **Our interpretations of the patterns of the past are projected into the expected patterns of the future.** The mind creates these maps to standardize our reactions. Life is way too complex to deal with each new situation in a new way. Without this futuring we could be frozen into relying only on instincts like animals. These maps guide and define our choices and behavior in the future. They are the road maps of what to expect and how to react as we travel through time.

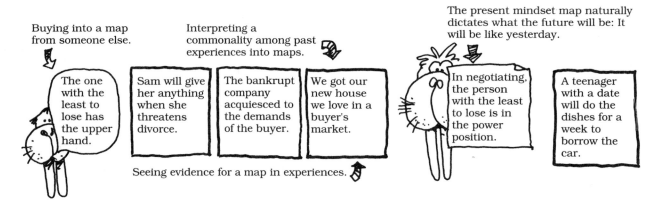

Buying into a map from someone else.

Interpreting a commonality among past experiences into maps.

The present mindset map naturally dictates what the future will be: It will be like yesterday.

The one with the least to lose has the upper hand.

Sam will give her anything when she threatens divorce.

The bankrupt company acquiesced to the demands of the buyer.

We got our new house we love in a buyer's market.

In negotiating, the person with the least to lose is in the power position.

A teenager with a date will do the dishes for a week to borrow the car.

Seeing evidence for a map in experiences.

Past

Present

Future

FLY SOUTH IN NOV.

Interpreting the experiences and creating a map explaining consistencies of the past, then projecting that map into predicting the future, creates an expectation of how things ought to be.

The mindset maps of the past give us the faith to accept tomorrow the faith that things are predictable and we can handle them.

Projecting into the Future

Humans are always using their mindset maps to predict the future, to know what is next week, tomorrow, or even what the next step will bring. We all are prophets. We predict the future. We use the maps we have acquired from others and our own experience to then project into guessing what the future will be like. These maps form our expectations. We expect things to work the same way they have in the past.

Life and its problems would be impossible and insane unless we can standardize our reactions with our mindset maps. This projecting our maps into the future saves our resources and attention for the new things that occasionally happen. We seldom expect them to be any different from yesterday. This ability is natural and a godsend for dealing with the complexities of life, but it may be a problem when it locks us into the solutions of the past.

- Everyone quietly predicts what grandma's reaction to the dinner will be. Sure enough, she tells everyone to eat their vegetables and have more.
- A brand new car just drove into the old automobile mechanic's shop. He sees the car's problem as the same kind of malfunction he has seen and fixed on much older cars.
- A foreign visitor to America wants to show his thanks for the nice meal his newfound friends made him and gives his culture's sign of appreciation for a well-prepared and served meal: He loudly belches.
- Janice expected her 20th class reunion to be like the memorable ones she heard her friends have—a reliving of the carefree and fun-filled days of high school.
- We grow up watching *Leave It To Beaver* and expect our family life to be the same.
- The father expected his sons to follow in his footsteps and run the business.
- When she got a flat tire on the freeway, Shirley expected some man to stop and fix her tire, especially after she raised the hood and looked helpless.
- Fendel assumes his mother will stay home, put on weight, have grey hair, be cheerful and bake cookies for her grandchildren.
- The economy will again rebound and the recession will end.

We use our maps like a tool kit of preconceived solutions to deal with tomorrow.

A map is like a tool kit we have created and boxed up to take with us into fixing situations in the future. By experience we have selected the best scewdriver, wrench and other tools to deal with the expected. And sure enough, the same things usually happen. We have to use the screwdriver on a similar screw just as we used yesterday. We have to use the same map on calming the boss as we did last week. We use the same tool the same way today as yesterday. We use the same map the same way today as yesterday.

49

Map Changing

Changing mindset maps changes our expectations and our reactions to the future. Creating a new map to again explain something when an old map fails to explain it seldom happens by itself, though. This change occurs when the old map gets us into trouble and no longer gets us what we expect and want. The change in maps happens when the old map simply doesn't work anymore. **We change maps when the pain and conflict of the old map not working makes our investment in it no longer worth it.**

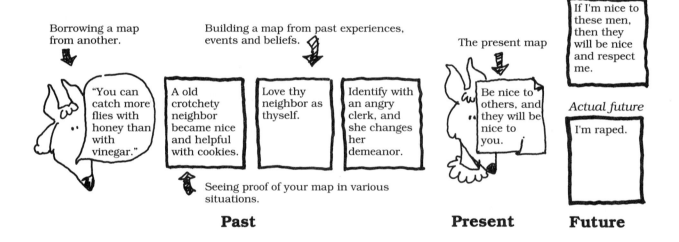

Borrowing a map from another.

"You can catch more flies with honey than with vinegar."

Building a map from past experiences, events and beliefs.

| A old crotchety neighbor became nice and helpful with cookies. | Love thy neighbor as thyself. | Identify with an angry clerk, and she changes her demeanor. |

Seeing proof of your map in various situations.

Past

The present map

Be nice to others, and they will be nice to you.

Present

Expected future

If I'm nice to these men, then they will be nice and respect me.

Actual future

I'm raped.

Future

A GOOD OCCUPATION IS TO BE IN HEALTH!

A GOOD OCCUPATION IS TO BE IN COMPUTERS

Any person viewing the world through his or her map expects the world to conform to that same map in the future. Expectations dictate what the responses will be. But when the future isn't what was expected, a conflict arises between the map and the reality. If the conflict is severe enough, the map changes or the person's responses will be inadequate.

What If Tomorrow Isn't What Was Expected?

A very natural expectation we all have is that the mindset maps we have that work well for us today will continue working in the future. But if the map doesn't work in the future and the map is thrown into conflict with the situation, then the map's owner is faced with the problem of resolving this conflict. The usual reaction to this problem is to adjust the map a little here and there, but believe the map will still function in providing order and predictability on how the world works. What worked today will still continue working tomorrow.

But what if our maps don't work the same tomorrow? What if the anticipated results aren't there? The map has worked well for years, but isn't now. The expected money isn't in the mail, the doctor couldn't do what he said he could, and the weather is the worst it has been in 140 years.

Difficulties arise when our anticipated future isn't the actuality. For example: You're ready to retire and the company's retirement fund will provide everything you need and want after the gold watch is presented on Thursday. But the company borrowed from the retirement fund and has filed for bankruptcy. Your expectations aren't working. When things like this happen, people tend to do the following things:

- **Ignore** the mismatch between what you expected and what happened. Make it disappear.
- **Make** the problem unimportant or insignificant. The problem of your map not working as expected isn't a problem. It's just a little thing and will go away shortly.
- **Pretend** it fits. There is a match and everything is all right. Make a fantasy land of illusions and pretense.
- **Force** it to fit. Make things work out with your expectation. Get others to help you. Extort evidence from anywhere you can supporting the old map. Demand that things work as predicted.
- **Attack** who or what may be causing the change. Find a scapegoat, a rope and a large tree.
- **Scan** the situation looking for the missing element—the one thing that you missed seeing which would explain why this obviously right and only solution won't work. It just has to be there!
- **Freeze**, shut down or opt out. Become helpless so you won't have to deal with it.
- **Change** the map. This is typically the last resort, and it almost always takes something or someone from outside the conflicting situation. Here is where a *Change Navigator* can be of the most help in getting another to see an alternative map. The starting point is when the pain quotient has been reached. The conflict between the mindset map and its expected results supersedes the investment in that map. And a new idea enters in—the map could be wrong.

"There is nothing permanent except change." Heraclitus 540-475 B.C. 51

Subliminal Map

The most important mindset maps you acquire are often unconscious or subliminally created. They are hidden maps. Many of our maps have come through our subconscious without conscious choice. We are not fully aware we are getting them and building them, and then using them to guide and direct our lives.

An example of three things in our life that taught us our maps on both a surface, or conscious, and hidden, or subliminal level: television, parents and history class:

TELEVISION
The average high school graduate has spent over 10,000 hours watching television.

Television Surface Level: **This show is entertainment. I can relax while I watch T V The nightly news is accurate and up-to-the-minute.**

Television Subliminal Level: **You can really understand complex problems with snipits of information on a regular daily basis from the nightly news. Life's problems can be solved in 30 to 60 minutes. Relationships are only superficial exchanges of critical humor. Violence solves problems. Life is to be experienced passively by watching other people's lives.**

PARENTS
Many people will probably receive many statements likes these your whole early life.

Parents' Surface Level: **Why don't you study more? I'm worried about you. You have little direction in your life. I'm very concerned about your future because of your behavior. I'm worried about the friends you pal around with.**

Parents' Subliminal Level: **Repeated exhortations of expected behavior will cause a change in that behavior. It is more loving to direct you over life's problems than to have you experience them yourself. My inadequate feelings and concerns over being a parent show in my constant badgering, and that is also how you must raise kids because that is how my parents raised me.**

HISTORY CLASS
May have to take history at least six to eight times in your life.

History Class Surface Level: **Knowing history will help make you an informed and involved citizen. The test on Chapter 5 will be on Tuesday. You got an "A" on the test—very good!**

History Class Subliminal Level: **A collection of names, dates and events is history. History is something to get over like chicken pox. History is boring and has no relationship to my life and what I'm doing.**

"Pornography affected my relationship with women. I treated them like things."
Duke University College Student

Surface

Buying these clothes will make you admired and accepted by your peers.

Buying this new style of clothes keeps our earnings up.

Hidden

Knowing what lies beneath the surface is usually unsettling. But not knowing it can keep you chained into being unable to respond with effectiveness and power.

Aware

We are here to teach and help you.

You are the excuse for our doing what we want.

Unaware

Our society and its various institutions can't take these subliminal maps coming to the surface. They often depend on these subliminal maps for control.

Most mindset maps are like something important hidden underwater. We are affected by them without knowing it. We take what is on the surface as being all there is. What is stated, or clearly seen and acknowledged, is all we must acknowledge and deal with. But like a boat sunk by a reef or submarine, failure to become aware of these hidden and subsurface maps in ourselves and others can affect, help, hurt, hinder or even sink us.

Subliminal Maps Dominate Our Lives

Many of our most important maps have come through our unconscious. These mindset maps are acquired through a subliminal process of repeated exposure. They may *never* be clearly stated, but subliminally taught by the people, environment and institutions in our life. We may not be fully aware that these hidden maps are guiding and dominating our lives.

I was once asked to assist with a Sunday school class for little children. The leaders and teachers in the class kept saying, "These classes are teaching our kids about God and being kind to their fellowman." "Good stuff," I thought. I had recently received as a gift one of those digital watches that does everything: slices, dices, purees; and it is a stop watch. So, as usually happens in places like this, my mind wanders and I started to time what was being said and done. What they said they were doing and what was really being done were two different things. It seems that over 90% of time what they were teaching the children was conformity. Conforming to the demands of the church leadership. It wasn't teaching about God; it had more to do with control. I quit after that. I honestly didn't see what was going on before I used the watch in timing what was really happening. Then it became obvious.

A number of years ago there was quite an uproar when people thought they were being brainwashed at the local movie theaters. People were convinced messages were being subliminally flashed on the screen in a fraction of a second to unsuspecting patrons. Its purported purpose was to have their subconscious buy more popcorn, pop and candy at the concession stand. Laws were enacted, people spoke out and the movie business was in some turmoil. There was nothing much to the entire issue; the whole thing was later dropped.

We have these subliminal maps taught all the time to us and our children, yet we fail to become uptight about any of it. They are very subtle and very effective manipulations and instructions. The most effective way to deal with these subliminal maps is to teach people to read them—make them come to the surface so they are not hidden any more. Seeing how certain hidden maps dictate our choices and reactions is critical to our survival, especially during these times of great change.

53

Governing Maps

If you had to keep track of all the mindset maps a person has, you could go crazy with the overload. But usually all you need to know are a few key ones such as the governing maps. **A governing map is the one map that dominates a whole set of other lesser maps.** It is like the main map in any atlas. For example, the map of the entire United States links together all the other subordinate state and city maps. A governing map is like the map which describes yourself and links to all the other subordinate relationship maps you may have with others.

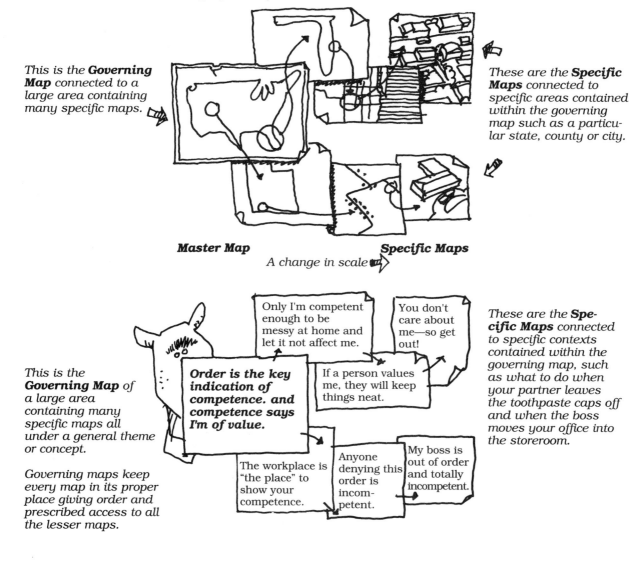

*This is the **Governing Map** connected to a large area containing many specific maps.*

*These are the **Specific Maps** connected to specific areas contained within the governing map such as a particular state, county or city.*

Master Map

Specific Maps

A change in scale

*This is the **Governing Map** of a large area containing many specific maps all under a general theme or concept.*

Governing maps keep every map in its proper place giving order and prescribed access to all the lesser maps.

Order is the key indication of competence. and competence says I'm of value.

Only I'm competent enough to be messy at home and let it not affect me.

You don't care about me—so get out!

If a person values me, they will keep things neat.

The workplace is "the place" to show your competence.

Anyone denying this order is incompetent.

My boss is out of order and totally incompetent.

*These are the **Specific Maps** connected to specific contexts contained within the governing map, such as what to do when your partner leaves the toothpaste caps off and when the boss moves your office into the storeroom.*

*Only one **Governing Map** may be the key to how most of a person's choices are made.*

The Secret to Change

People have a few master or *Governing Maps* that direct large areas of their lives. Within these large areas are the collections of subordinate or lesser maps. Where the total number of mindset maps a person uses could easily be in the tens of thousands, governing maps are only a few. But those few consistently dominate most of the decisions people make.

To work more effectively with people and institutions, helping them to adapt to change, you need to know their governing maps. They are like windows into what and how their important choices are made. You have a much better chance of change by understanding, acknowledging and utilizing these maps than in any other way.

How and why they got this particular map isn't important. Many people believe that to cause change you must know why this map came to be. Searching for why a map came about is wasted effort often leading to unanswerable questions which, even if known, wouldn't change anything. Their mother may have diapered the wrong end or they may have been attacked by a breakfast cereal as a kid, but it doesn't help you change their viewpoints. What the map is is much more important because it dictates the responses of today, in the here and now.

A Metaphor That Governs Choice

The governing map is often a central metaphor. A whole company may be into a football metaphor with statements like, "The long bomb into the end zone, or protect your quarterback." A salesman may use the metaphor of a western gunslinger with comments like, "Shooting from the hip, staring down the competition, and shooting oneself in the foot." A Japanese manufacturing company's governing map is to, "make the goods flow like water into one continuous flow of raw materials, then into preassembled parts, finally ending with a sold product." An American manufacturer has a map of separate steps leading to a finished product on the top step. The holistic view of manufacturing, with the map of water flowing, may be more beneficial in making production more efficient.

*If you want to deal with this organization and affect any change, you must acknowledge this **Governing Map**.*

If you can know the *Governing Map*, a lot of options to affect change fall into view, but institutions and people can also become very vulnerable. For example, a corporation I know sees itself as favored by God. The unique founding and growth of the company verify this; behind closed doors in executive meetings they often talk of God's provident hand, and they use the metaphor of being, "a beacon for the Lord." A salesman, seeing this need of divine acceptance, packaged a computer presentation with words and mannerisms indicating God had sent him. They bought everything he presented, including hiring the salesman. The computer had to be replaced within a year, but the salesman is still there.

55

Map Confirmation

When people have an important mindset map, they automatically seek confirmation that it is correct or valid. They search for proof or evidence in their interactions to support the map's validity. People act like a scientist, searching for support for his hypothesis throughout his experiences and in experiments that he conducts. This map confirmation is a common activity people spend a large share of their time and energy doing. The more important the map, the more time is spent on seeking its confirmation, especially seeking confirmation that the personal map of themselves is accurate.

Showing various contexts confirming a person's particular mindset map.

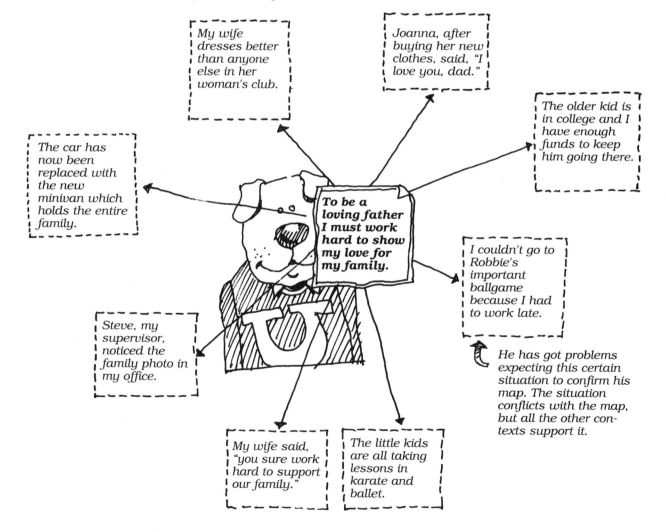

Confirming the Correctness of a Mindset Map

People confirm their mindset map's correctness through evidence gathering. They match the proof they find in life to the map they've created. They strive for harmony between the map they own and the surrounding environment, with both the territory and the map saying the same thing. Like with a regular map, you know it is correct because the map matches the terrain. Where the map says there will be a mountain, there it is in front of you, and where the map shows a bridge over the river, there it is under your car wheels. The more the map matches the actual territory, the more confirmation supporting the accuracy of the map. The same with both an actual map and a mindset map. Here are a few examples:

We confirm the accuracy of a road map by matching it against the actual territory. The same with a mindset map.

- Jake has a map which states, "people who are geniuses are often absentminded and incoherent." The professor's rambling lecture with his fly open confirms he must be brilliant.
- Candice's map is "if at first you don't succeed, you try, try again," typically called *The Little Engine That Could* map. After repeated tries, she finally passes the bar exam—the map is confirmed.
- Steven's using an office pencil at home confirms Leigh's map of moral superiority. She feels, "If he is a thief in that, he probably is a thief in other larger things and I can't trust him."
- The corporation has a map that M.B.A.s are the best ones to manage the firm. So they let go and retired any employees without this degree. But they can't get the map confirmed because with the lack of hands-on experience of the new M.B.A.s the prior efficiency level drastically drops throughout the company.
- Wally has a map that determines he is a scum bucket and not worth much. Then the fact Sue, his friend, calls him "an obnoxious nerd!" confirms his map. The terrain verifies the map's correctness.
- May has determined on her map that she is the best for the new position opening up at work. But the company president refuses her advancement to vice president. May's map has the evidence that either it is inaccurate, he can't really see her true worth, or possibly the president is discriminating against her as a woman. She will now have to either modify the map or reinterpret the evidence.

Modifying and Updating the Map

People make modifications and updates on their maps from the discrepancies they receive in this confirming process. If their map is inaccurate someplace, a correction can be made. The actual territory with the real landmarks should preempt any map of that same territory. What is really there should dominate any decisions over what should or ought to be there.

But when we have invested heavily in the map's accuracy and correctness, especially if it must be absolutely correct, this entire confirming process distorts. The process turns into only seeking validation or positive proof. Anything against it is ignored, blocked and even eliminated. Confirming can easily turn into only validating when the map is more important than any contrary evidence.

57

Need Wheel

We all seek to have our needs fulfilled. Unmet needs are our motivating force. We all have the need to be loved, to be competent, to be safe, etc. **Our needs provide the power pushing us all towards fulfilling them, and the mindset maps give that power a direction.** A feeling of being unsafe motivates a person to seek safety, but a map which states "unpredictability is unsafe, and public places are unpredictable" may move the fulfillment of that need in a specific direction. For example, this person stays out of crowded or public places.

The number of needs and their particular names and descriptions often vary and depend on what expert you're talking to, but it is a fact that we all have inherent needs and they are the critical factor in motivating us. The *Need Wheel* shows how the eight individual needs remain balanced and in harmony with each other, but when one need is left chronically unmet, more and more personal resources are spent in satisfying it.

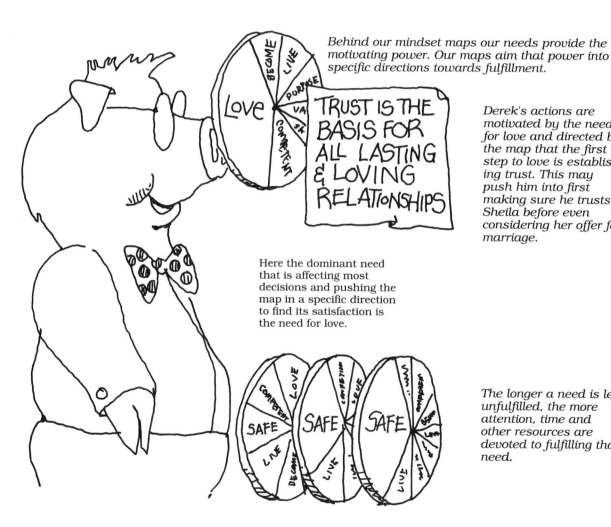

Behind our mindset maps our needs provide the motivating power. Our maps aim that power into specific directions towards fulfillment.

Derek's actions are motivated by the need for love and directed by the map that the first step to love is establishing trust. This may push him into first making sure he trusts Sheila before even considering her offer for marriage.

Here the dominant need that is affecting most decisions and pushing the map in a specific direction to find its satisfaction is the need for love.

The longer a need is left unfulfilled, the more attention, time and other resources are devoted to fulfilling that need.

The need provides the power as with a car engine, and the map directs that power as with the steering wheel.

A person's most unmet need with its accompanying map will dominate most of his or her actions and choices.

This person is motivated by feeling love.

This person is pushed into various choices by the need to be competent.

And this person is motivated by the need to meet his or her physical needs such as food, sleep and air.

The Power Behind the Map

The purpose of life is fulfillment—meeting our inner needs. Psychologists say that the driving force behind all human activity is the fulfillment of needs. Here is a list what most people categorize into the basic needs:

• We want to **Live**. These are the physical needs such as food, air, water, the right temperature, health, etc. When denied, we could die if these needs are unmet.

• We want to **Love**, and **Be Loved** in return. Infants denied human contact may die. Human beings are social beings needing a partner and friends who care and who can be cared for.

• We need a sense of **Belonging** to someone and something, to be accepted into something more than ourselves, such as a relationship, an organization or a belief.

• We want a **Purpose** in our lives, a reason for being, a sense that we have a place in the larger order of things and that our existence means something.

• We want to **Become** more. More than we are now. We want to grow and progress.

• We want to **Feel Important**, respect for who and what we are. We want people to value us in some way. We desire impact on something and someone in making a difference.

• We want to have **Variety.** We want to have experiences in life, to interact with new people, ideas, things and situations.

• We want to be **Competent** in the things we do. We seek for expression and the ability to do it well.

• We want to be **Safe** within our physical and social environment. We want to be secure in our person and in our place from both physical and emotional harm.

The need list that you would create may be different than this one; it doesn't matter, the need wheel will function the same. Whatever need is chronically left unmet will dominate over all the other needs. For example, people who are very unsafe aren't usually thinking of the need for variety or competence. Also, if you get some food caught in your throat and your air supply is blocked, you may not be thinking of the importance of impressing the other people at the table. If you are, you may be dead.

The basic needs of a person cannot be questioned. They are the way they are. They are factual states of being. A lot of time and effort is wasted on trying to change another's needs because their behavior seems undesirable. With this understanding of mindset maps, if you can change their maps, redirecting the motivating power of their dominant need, you can change their behavior. This way acknowledges the need and works on the map. People always behave consistently with their maps. Changing maps changes behavior.

The Personal Map

The most important of all the governing maps is the personal map. **It the map that usually governs all the rest of the other maps.** An individual's entire atlas of maps is linked and subordinate to this single central map. The personal map defines who we are. This map determines a person's position, role and actions in all the relationships he or she has to things such as people, ideas, the environment, even to their own selves—to everything. Everyone needs to know where he or she is before it can determined where everything else is.

A *Personal Map* gives definition and position for its owner in all his or her relationships to everything else. This map shows how to relate physically, emotionally, financially, culturally, socially and spiritually to everyone else.

This is the map that tells us where we are in relationship to everthing else.

The actual person.

The personal map of the person.

The Dominant Map

The *Personal Map* literally rules and regulates our lives. It soaks through and permeates every aspect of our life, coloring everything we think and do. The degree of reality in this one map determines our success in meeting this changing world more than anything else. If false, our reactions and all other maps are tainted by its errors. Here is an example of a personal map dominating a life:

Sidney is chief mechanical engineer in the research and development department at a large manufacturing firm. He has a personal map that pictures himself as the important center to what is going on in his personal and especially his work environment. The firm he works for considers itself to be at the leading edge of technology, and Sidney considers himself to be at the leading edge within the firm. Around the office and at home you can often hear him saying things like, "This area I'm now working on will change the face of business," or he will whisper, "Some important new research is leading to a tremendous new breakthrough, but you must swear to secrecy if I tell you."

The teenage years are focused on developing and filling in our personal maps. Once somewhat completed, teenagers can get onto someone else other than themselves and into other realtionships.

Everything was going along fine until another engineer, not even in the same department, made a crucial breakthrough which was felt could change the entire direction of the firm. The limelight Sidney had enjoyed shifted to an engineer named Duane. Sidney went bonkers. All he said and did from then on was centered on putting Duane into a bad light. Sidney would say, "It was faulty research. Duane is inept and not qualified." He even blamed Duane for "stealing the idea from the Japanese." It became a continual barrage of negative comments to lessen Duane's important contribution.

Finally, to complicate things even further, Duane's daughter had married Sidney's son just before all this got started. The daughter-in-law even became a point of all the insinuating comments. Before, she was fine for their son, even desirable by being in the same business. Now Sidney's entire family was orchestrated into demeaning and even eliminating her from the family. Things were getting rough.

Anyone very close threatens me so I must keep my distance to be safe.

*The **Personal Map**, more than any other map, must be stable and healthly in order to effectively interact with others.*

Sidney's need was importance, with a teaspoon of the need for competence mixed in, and his personal map of being number one directed it towards this attack against Duane. This contest dominated his life and his attention for a whole year until Duane moved on to another firm and he again regained his position. Harmony with his map was restored.

Guiding Us in All Our Choices

Our personal maps direct our choices more than anything else. They are key in understanding what our reactions to things will be because they are always consistent with our personal map. Any *Change Navigator* should understand this and use it as the key to causing the needed changes to handle change itself.

Group Maps

A group can share a common or single mindset map. Organizations and institutions can be so in unison about some specific belief or viewpoint that they function as a single individual. People may support, pressure and control each other within the group to keep everyone in line with a common frame of mind towards meeting the group needs over any single person's needs.

*Here is a single map
shared by a group.*

*People who share a
common map tend to
act, look and think
alike.*

Insiders

*Large maps often are
held in place by wheels.*

Outsider

*Conflicting mindset
maps*
often lead to conflict.

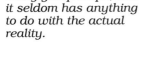

Our personal feelings and emotions have nothing to do with the decision making process within the corporation.

This is a common statement written on many group maps, but it seldom has anything to do with the actual reality.

Sharing a Mindset Map

People share the same map when they come together in groups. These shared maps are the commonality that binds these groups into cohesive units. Such groups can be formal or informal, and can range from families to unions and from companies to nations.

Think about a group to which you belong. Do members of your group share the same beliefs, values and ideas? These shared concepts are the elements that bind your group and other groups together. Just like traveling on a journey with other people when everyone follows and makes choices from the same map. A shared mindset map is common in all groups, organizations and institutions.

Every group has their shared maps that is what makes them a group. Some examples of organizational map sharing:

GROUP: **Nazi Germany**
GOVERNING PRINCIPLE SUMMARIZING A GROUP MAP: Man is a creature to be bred for quality to rule the world for a 1,000 year reign.
RESULTS: During the final battles of World War II, troop trains are stopped so that trains carrying "subhumans" to the concentration camps can get through.

People within a group may not value any beliefs from outside their shared map.

GROUP: **Moslem Fundamentalists**
GOVERNING PRINCIPLE SUMMARIZING A GROUP MAP: Allah will eventually triumph over all, and dying for the cause will take you directly to heaven.
RESULTS: Thousands of poorly trained Iranian youth die in mass attack against the Iraqi army.

GROUP: **The Rosten Family**
GOVERNING PRINCIPLE SUMMARIZING A GROUP MAP: You kiss those you love and you always love relatives.
RESULTS: Two weeks after the yearly family reunion everyone mysteriously comes down with the flu.

GROUP: **U.S.A.**
GOVERNING PRINCIPLE SUMMARIZING A GROUP MAP: We must be the world's policeman.
RESULTS: Korea, Cuba, Vietnam, Lebanon, Grenada, Panama, Iraq, Somalia, Balkans, etc.

GROUP: **Norman and Ilene Muller**
GOVERNING PRINCIPLE SUMMARIZING A GROUP MAP: Family always takes care of family.
RESULTS: After their son Brad died, his parents and the other siblings with their mates rushed to his wife, Diana's side in Ohio, with emotional and financial support.

GROUP: **Church of the Holy Communion With the Lord**
GOVERNING PRINCIPLE SUMMARIZING GROUP MAP: The Lord will only help those who give up all they have to Him and He seeks a sign of that sacrifice.
RESULTS: Larry and Marge deeded all they have to the church and the Most Reverend Conrad T. Tillage.

We are all affected by this group's map.

63

The Opposing Map

Any mindset map that has a principle, belief, idea, ideal or concept written on its surface is always linked to its contrasting opposite. A map's opposite is automatically connected to it because it is innate in the way ideas and thinking works. You can't have any idea without its contrasting opposite.

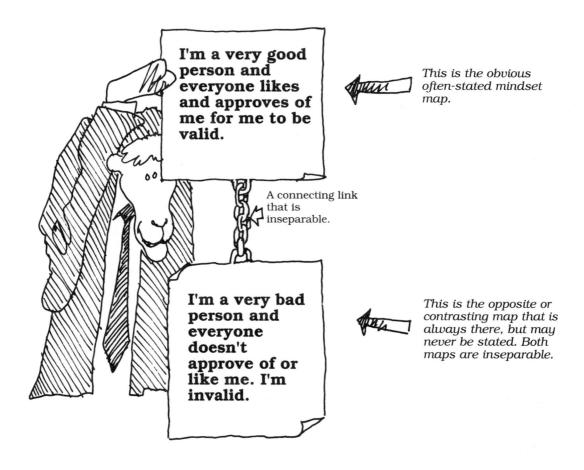

I'm a very good person and everyone likes and approves of me for me to be valid.

This is the obvious often-stated mindset map.

A connecting link that is inseparable.

I'm a very bad person and everyone doesn't approve of or like me. I'm invalid.

This is the opposite or contrasting map that is always there, but may never be stated. Both maps are inseparable.

The Mindset Map and Its Contrasting Companion—A Pair of Siamese Twins

Whatever principle, idea, concept or belief that is adopted into the mindset map has its opposite that is also automatically connected. This linking of a mindset map with its contrasting opposite is always the case. It is innate in the way ideas and thinking work. You can't understand anything without understanding its opposite. The concept of stop is connected with the concept of don't stop, pain linked to pleasure, righteousness with evil, approval with disapproval, competence with incompetence, and so on. Two opposing personalities are inseparably connected and in a continual dynamic and natural tug-of-war between the two. If the map has what a successful businessman is, it also has fastened to it what an unsuccessful businessman is. If someone has that he or she is no good at math written on his or her map, they also have linked to the map what being good at math means. Any comparison and measuring couldn't be done without the juxtaposition between these contrasting opposites. To illustrate, here is a list of contrasting and opposing maps:

I must suffer for my mystakes.

My suffering is useless.

I'm competent when . . .

I'm incompetent when . . .

Our mindset maps are really two maps: the obvious open one on the surface and the hidden deeper one. The latter map is often feared and seldom, if ever, stated.

- A company has the idea on its collective map that it exists only to turn consistent and continual profits. When the losses mount and won't abate, the company may find its collective self staring at the idea that the company has no reason to continue being in existence. This may lead to frantic behavior to increase those profits, almost ruthless decisions where they are facing life and death, and if the losses continue, even fatalism. But all these actions could block reactions that would be the best responses for the future. The problem is that in adopting the limited and absolute mindset of continued profits for survival, this organization also adopted its opposite as absolute.

- The belief that the majority rules contain within it the fact that the minority doesn't. In order for the majority not to overpower and completely dominate the minority, other concepts have to be mapped out so the minority is protected against the whims of the majority.

- April has a map that she exists only for her family. She has spent the last 30 years of marriage serving her husband and children. Everything she does or says revolves around them. But now in the last few years her kids have gone, the old battle between the two boys has resurfaced in adulthood, and her husband has just told her he has had an affair. April wants to die.

- "Better made products like ours last longer. This increases the desirability of our products over our competition, and we dominate this very stable market. But our products, once in place, remain there, working without maintenance and repair for many years, and our customers don't need to buy from us again for a very long time. They are very satisfied, but our sales and profits aren't. What brought us the sales in the first place has now stopped us dead."

The real issue is most often the space between these contrasting maps.

- This idea of opposing maps is important later when you get into reading maps. The real map which directs a person's life is often the opposite of the map that he or she may state he or she has.

65

The Map Box

Every map comes in its own box. **Each mindset map is a representation of the outside world, but this map also superimposes its description onto its surroundings and creates a world or box of its own.** The map is seen as the world or part of it. This is a natural tendency of all maps. They tend to become viewed as the territory they represent. The representation is seen as real, and it creates expectations dictating order and responses onto the outside reality. **This _Map Box_ is the world through which every mindset map is expressed and through which it can be reached by the navigator.**

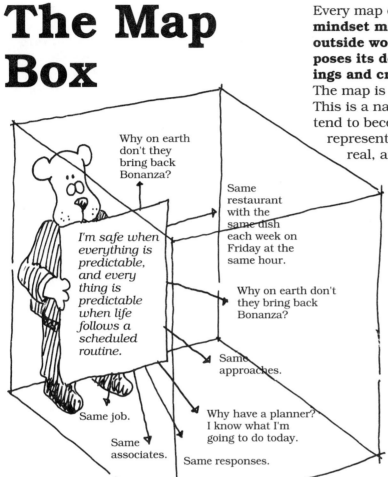

Why on earth don't they bring back Bonanza?

Same restaurant with the same dish each week on Friday at the same hour.

I'm safe when everything is predictable, and every thing is predictable when life follows a scheduled routine.

Why on earth don't they bring back Bonanza?

Same approaches.

Same job.

Same associates.

Why have a planner? I know what I'm going to do today.

Same responses.

For example, this person's crucial need is in being safe, and his mindset map is centered on predictability as being the way to this safety. The box constructed around his map matches everything against it in terms of being predictable. Same job for 30 years, doing the same thing the same way with the same people. Anything unpredictable is rejected as unsafe and pushed out of his world.

The walls of the box are hard or soft depending on how much is invested in making sure whatever the map says is true.

Soft, open walls, perforated and permeable; things can change and modify, new ideas accepted.

Harder walls, anything outside the box is increasingly harder to be absorbed or enter in; modifications and changes rejected.

Very hard walls, concrete and steel, nothing allowed in or out; new ideas are a threat, a prison and a fortress.

Things should be fair here, but in this case I would rather not have any problems. I'll give it up.

A map of fairness in one person's world may have walls that are flexible and adaptable, but with another person, even with the same map but with more invested, it may be all inclusive and so important they would fight for adherance to their map.

Things should be fair here, and if you don't give me what I deserve, I'll turn it over to my lawyer and let the courts make you be fair.

The Box the Mindset Map Comes In

Each map has a set area enveloping it. **A mindset map creates a box or world around it.** This world or box is brought on through the support, application and investment into the mindset map. The more involved in the map its owners are and invested into its continuation, the more defined and stronger the walls of the box are. The walls could vary from being very permeable to absolutely closed, not allowing even light or air in. The walls of the box can be like a misty cloud, or like a wire cage, or maybe something very closed like a terrarium, with its own separate little world. Here are some examples of the box-like worlds created by the mindset maps at their center:

• Pilot Chuck Yeager piloted the first aircraft through the sound barrier in October of 1947 and entered the age of supersonic flight. This speed-of -sound barrier was an "invisible brick wall." Some scientists had built a mindset map of "hard data" that it was impenetrable. If this wall was shattered, it was believed the pilot could lose his voice, revert in age, and the airplane would be severely vibrated into disintegrating. Three weeks later Yeager piloted the Bell Aviation X-1 plane into twice the speed of sound, forever breaking down the walls of this sound barrier box. Could our concept of the speed of light be contained within similar walls?

• This 5th grade teacher teaches evolution. But it has become more than a study in science; it has become her cause. She talks about it in all her classes even though it is not the subject matter being taught. All her field trips are centered around it; she champions evolution at the smallest opportunity. She lives and breathes it; it is her life and her love. When another teacher questions her on this, she is immediately called "a creationist" and made an enemy of her cause.

• The foundation's acting president, Colonel Frampton, is obsessed with maintaining the good image of the foundation at all costs. He was blackmailed by a reporter who had researched into the foundation's shady history, and in order to stop him from making it public, payed him thousands of dollars. He instructed all area directors to threaten with firing any employee having direct contact with the public media. All press releases had to be personally supervised by the colonel. When a top vice president was "let go" because he was caught with his hand in the foundation's till, he made the comment, "It wouldn't look good for the foundation's image to have this in the papers." The foundation's need was survival; its map was that a pure public image was critical to that survival, and the president zealously made an airtight box around it.

• A mechanical all-inclusive world of physics was neatly packaged by the brilliant Isaac Newton into a box containing all the laws of force and gravity. Like a fine-tuned wind-up clock, it ran very well for years, re-placed when the world needed more and Albert Einstein proposed his revolutionary ideas of time, space, speed and gravity.

This map box is what makes it so hard to see any outside alternative. The map inside may be very flawed, but because it only allows inside the box ideas which fit its parameters, it tends to defeat its needed replacement.

Your Mindset Map

We have all brought certain approaches, principles, attitudes and ideas and put them into our individual mindset maps. We may also have invested a good deal of time, effort, money, ego and the like in believing that these maps are right. But is it possible that some of these maps of yours need correction and updating or may even need to be entirely replaced? **You may have mindset maps with some things written on them that are incorrect!**

Making what is written on your map visible and out in the open is the first step to seeing and measuring what is there.

Looking at our own maps is very hard to do, especially when many of us don't even know we have one and those few of us that do have never really looked at ours. But this introspection is critical in dealing with change.

Seeing Your Own Maps

We all have mindset maps in front of our faces guiding all our choices. We look at them to see the world and make sense of it. Just knowing that fact can give us a considerable amount of power, both over our own actions and in understanding the actions of others. Seeing our own beliefs, principles and explanations drawn on our map, and the degree to which they dictate who we are and how we act, can be both a severe shock and a life-changing experience.

In examining my own mindset map and trying to identify the principles and beliefs on how to get what I want written on it, I have discovered that more than half of my rules or principles were incorrect. My conversations with others show that percentage to be fairly consistent across the board.

Change the Map and We Change Who We Are and What We Can and Cannot Do

What is written on our maps defines who we are, how we act and what we may become. Our individual and group successes in life depend on our seeing life through a mindset map having more accurate principles and routes drawn on it. Incorrect material on the map leaves us lost in chaos and brings us face-to-face with our nightmares. A map with material that is true and in line with how things really are helps us to go where we need to and reach our dreams.

Key Points About Your Own Mindset Maps:

• *What is written on your maps defines your future.*

• *It is possible for you to change your maps.*

• *Behavior is changed when a person adopts a map.*

• *The most important mindset maps are the ones you have invested the most in being true.*

• *It is possible that half of your maps may be false.*

The biggest problem of map making is not that we have to start from scratch, but that if our maps are to be accurate we have to continually revise them. The world itself is constantly changing. Glaciers come, glaciers go. Cultures come, cultures go. There is too little technology, there is too much technology. Even more dramatically, the vantage point from which we view the world is constantly and quite rapidly changing. When we are children we are dependent, powerless. As adults we may be powerful. Yet in illness or an infirm old age we may become powerless and dependent again. When we have children to care for, the world looks different from when we have none; when we are raising infants, the world seems different from when we are raising adolescents. When we are poor, the world looks different from when we are rich. We are daily bombarded with new information as to the nature of reality. If we are to incorporate this information, we must continually revise our maps, and sometimes when enough new information has accumulated, we must make very major revisions. The process of making revisions, particularly major revisions, is painful, sometimes excruciatingly painful. And herein lies the source of many of the ills of mankind."

M. Scott Peck
A Road Less Traveled

See How You Are Seeing

Making what is written on your map visible and out in the open is the first step to seeing and measuring what is there. You can't evaluate, improve or admire anything about the map unless you know what it is and can see it clearly. Write down or draw out what is written on your most important maps. You may need someone you can trust, be safe with, and who can be objective with you to help you to do this. You may be very surprised if you have never done this before. Just knowing what your own governing maps really are can often cause dramatic changes in your life.

Looking at our own maps is very hard to do, especially when many of us don't even know we have one and those few of us that do have never really looked at ours. But this introspection is critical in dealing with change. Every time I've done this, I've found errors in thinking on my maps, and everyone I've helped to see his or her governing maps reports the same. This map reading may be best done on others first before tackling yourself. It is usually a lot easier to look at others than ourselves. Seeing their maps clearly can only help us see our own. The next section is on reading maps and how to do it.

Two Kinds of Seeing the World

There are two kinds of people in this world: those who let their senses and perceptions override their maps and those who don't. The vast majority of people are in the latter group. They are locked into looking at only their maps instead of seeing what is actually happening around them. Their maps dictate their reactions and behavior over the reality of the situation. The commands of their maps override any conflicting input from their senses. They are not in real time, but in a kind of map time where they blindly follow the symbols and words on the paper over the dirt, rain and rock they are walking in. The drawing of a mountain takes precedence over any real mountain. The line on the map for a road is followed over the real asphalt they are driving on.

There are two kinds of people in this world:

Those who see the world as it is.

And those who see only their map of the world.

Dealing with the first group, who see beyond their map, is no problem. The navigator does it directly, openly and to the point. Since they are usually already seeing what is needed and adapting anyway, he is typically working with them in record time. Loneliness among this kind is common, and anyone who sees the changes is often clearly welcome as a comrade and helper. But to deal with the other group is another matter. The navigator needs to read their map, and because they follow it like a robot, he or she knows how they will react—as their map dictates they should. He can then determine a route around or through them, maybe even helping them choose to change to a more accurate map. The first group tends to follow what they perceive; the last group just reads and follows their map.

Fitting into Both Groups

Ron was a very capable design consultant to the same firm I also worked with. We were both working in the same office.

One day he physically grabbed me as I headed for the president's office, stared straight into my eyes and said, "I'm tired of you! I'm as good of a designer as you, even better, and I demand to know what you are up to. You come into this office and proceed to interact with top management. You don't go through the channels on a tight schedule as I have to." He continued, pointing to rather standardized work he was doing in the corner of a side office, "I'm stuck here in this back room working on these silly drawings while you hob-nob with the top." Ron's frustration level had reached the point where he had had enough of his perceived lowly position in the company and wanted more. He wanted to know what I was doing to be involved where I was.

Ron had a typical mindset that many designers have. Design was a superior activity done by superior people. He believed he was superior because he was a designer. Design is a higher calling involving a higher art than the mundane activities the rest of us do. Ron was a high priest knowing the secrets of this high calling—above mere mortals. And others, including management—a lower calling—were to respect this.

I gave him the process of mindset mapping and how mindsets determine one's value within an organization. Finding the key people's mindset map within the organization, such as the president, lets you know what they value. Then exchanging what you want for what they want gives you value. With map reading you reflect back to the key people within an organization what is written on their maps as being of value. This translates into you being better rewarded for the work you do with position, access, income, etc. Ron had assumed that there was just some absolute high standard of financial remuneration for his innately superior design work.

Unknown to Ron, he was being talked about in those high offices he wanted to enter. The company executives were considering letting him go, but then Ron did something miraculous. I've never seen such a rapid change in a person in such a short time. He ended up in the executive offices with me. And with the other accounts Ron had there was a very dramatic increase in income and work load. This all happened in a matter of a couple of months. I even found myself envious and wondering why I had ever told him.

His new level of thinking in mindset maps and exchanging value went along for a few more months. Then something happened. He let go of the power he had demanded and received. His work slid back to the old way of doing things. Ron was moved back to the back room and finally out the door.

My curiosity got me to talk with him about what had happened. "Those bastards have no respect for good work," he replied, talking about the company leadership. "All they want is money and more money. They don't have the aesthetic sense of a rock." Through others in the office I also heard what he thought of me. "My stupid idea about maps could be expected from a person with his head so far up you know where." He turned very bitter and resentful. The last time I heard from him he was stuck in a job in some back room somewhere.

Why did Ron let go of the power he said he wanted? I suppose it would take some psychologist years of therapy with him to find out for sure. I think it had something to do with Ron wanting the idealistic map of his innate superiority to be real more than he wanted to pay the price of power and let go of the idealistic map and also accept the entire concept of maps. The mindset map idea threatened Ron's entire belief that his perception is not set and absolute. He was demanding that he didn't possess a map of reality—his view of things was reality.

"The map is not the territory."
Alfred Korzybski

Map Reading

Discerning Another's Mindset Map to Facilitate Change

This is a warning! What follows in the next sections can easily be misused and should be handled with great care.

A great deal of very positive things have happened to me because of this entire navigating process, but I feel you should also know about the problems. You may avoid my pitfalls by simply asking yourself a few questions.

I share with you this process as a tool for you to use in helping others and yourself adapt to change. I wish all intentions to be good. But there is often a hazy line between manipulating and helping. I hope you can find the line. I had some rough times when I didn't. With a zealous ineptitude, I hurt some people I care deeply about; I gave them insights that they were too fragile to deal with. Now as I look back, I was more showing off than empowering them. A woman once apologized for getting mad at me. Then she said, "I felt naked before you." I had said nothing, but somehow she knew that I could read her to her very center. This is a lot of power. Consideration for sensitive feelings should always be taken into account. So I advise you, up front, take great care in learning and applying what follows. It can be a heady experience in knowing how to see where others are blind. This brings us to the first question: **Is your intention right?** And the next question: **Can the people you're interacting with stand the insights into their situations that discernment brings, and if so, who are you to give it to them?**

I've seen many individuals use materials similar to what is in this book to manipulate those around them. Judd uses what he reads on his friends' and associates' maps to enlarge his wallet. He simply uses his discernment of their maps to milk people of their money. Sometimes it is their life savings. Many still consider him their friend and speak kindly of him even when he whispers how dumb and blind they are. Judd often says, "I give them what they want and are hungry for, and they give me what I want, money—an even trade."

So, I also decided to use *Map Reading* as a way of protection. I figured that if others had this knowledge, they couldn't be so easily manipulated. Give them protection against the sharks. Sounds good, doesn't it? But it is harder to draw the line, and it isn't as good or as easy as it sounds.

My Dr. Frankenstein Stories

A common problem with this *Map Reading* process is that once you read another's map and know what he or she is really up to, you can't easily pretend you don't see it. Where before you were unaware, now you see the game being played, and it is an extreme temptation to tell others what you see. But doing this can make being a *Change Navigator* a dangerous job. For example, I gave this process to a friend and colleague. He later developed the ability to read his wife's and her relative's maps. He saw for the first time their joint manipulations over his life. He then called them all on their manipulations that they were playing on him. The game, which had lasted for many years, was over. His wife, realizing this, went crazy. She went into a rampage, attacking me in every way possible short of physical violence and even threatened that. His world dramatically changed. He is now very happily remarried, but I'm still occasionally the fading target for his former wife's anger. It seems my friend had blamed me for his new insight. It became my fault he could see the game and left the marriage.

Map reading can be a two-edged sword where it can provide you with power over situtations, but unintentionally you may hurt others. Truth can cause pain.

Still another story to illustrate: I watched as a department head destroyed a very successful program within his department. It was all done under such high-sounding phrases as, "We all need the resources devoted to this program put into critical future development. This program doesn't meet the purpose of this company. And, we don't have the finances to support this program (it was always profitable)." All these statements and actions hid the real reason. He was intensely jealous of this program, the limelight and the resources it brought to the person directing it. I simply showed the program director what the department head was doing (Dumb move). I thought I was helping the program continue. But this program wasn't his real issue, his security was. The program director told the department head, and, again under high-sounding phrases, I was fired. This brings us to the next rule: **Do the individuals you're dealing with show a pattern of not accepting responsibility and blaming others?**

I've found it a good general rule to keep what you read on another's map to yourself and, as much as possible, be silent about the whole change-navigating process (shut-up! in other words).

I'm giving you all these stories with their questions to try to save you from being as dumb as I was. These few questions have since saved my hide and my conscience many times. I learned them the hard way; I hope you don't have to. Now, on into the process.

Seeing the Invisible

What follows is a more detailed look at mindset maps and how people make decisions using them as their guides. The purpose here is to read others, mindset maps so you can better deal with them, especially in situations that require immediate insight and quick responses. This section is not on altering maps that will be the next section. This section is on reading another's map or a group's maps to determine how you can best interact with them.

Map Reading is the ability to *see* the consistency behind people's choices. It is *seeing* how people make decisions from their mindset map which causes them to respond in certain ways. **An invisible mindset map becomes visible when this pattern of underlying consistency behind their actions resulting from certain choices becomes apparent.**

Affecting change in another first begins in knowing his or her present position. Knowing another's mindset map can provide the needed information for the *Change Navigator* to adjust his or her actions in dealing with them. Where most people are flying blind in interacting with others, the navigator will be able to see clearly their location and direction. Here is an example of the basic concept of *Map Reading*:

The Change Navigator
The navigator's primary job is to first read and plot his or her present position from the mindset map of the individuals or groups he or she is working with.

Navigators read another's map by observing the consistency in their actions.

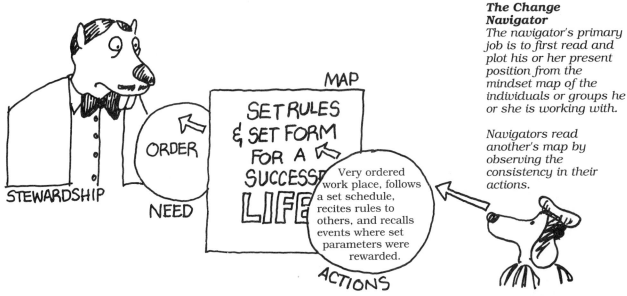

Stewardship
The navigator's shipmates or those he or she is responsible for in assisting in navigating through change. This may be a single person, a group of people or an entire organization.

The Need Wheel
The motivating and moving power behind the map that is innate within the person.

Mindset Map
The guide which directs the need towards fulfillment and from which the choices are made that direct the actions.

Behavior/ Actions
This is the only thing you can really see; all else is hidden within the individual. Choices determine actions, and maps direct the choices.

The Route
This is the course navigators plot out to take them from their present position with their stewardship to their final location with them.

The Underlying Consistency

People act consistently with their personal mindset map. Reading this underlying consistency in another's behavior constitutes your interpretation of his or her personal map. These patterns can often be summarized into a single simple statement. Then with this statement you can predict with accuracy how individuals will react in specific situations. Though not 100% accurate, it is often surprising how well map reading works.

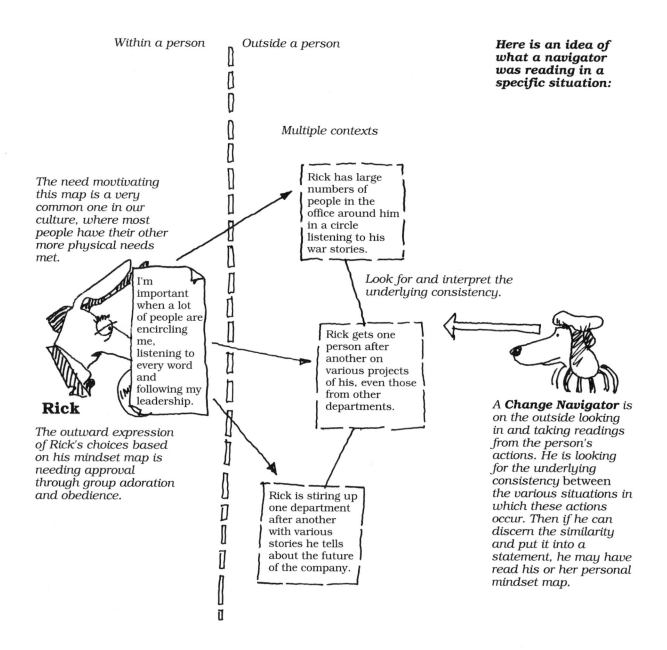

Within a person

Outside a person

Here is an idea of what a navigator was reading in a specific situation:

Multiple contexts

The need motivating this map is a very common one in our culture, where most people have their other more physical needs met.

Rick has large numbers of people in the office around him in a circle listening to his war stories.

I'm important when a lot of people are encircling me, listening to every word and following my leadership.

Look for and interpret the underlying consistency.

Rick

The outward expression of Rick's choices based on his mindset map is needing approval through group adoration and obedience.

Rick gets one person after another on various projects of his, even those from other departments.

*A **Change Navigator** is on the outside looking in and taking readings from the person's actions. He is looking for the underlying consistency between the various situations in which these actions occur. Then if he can discern the similarity and put it into a statement, he may have read his or her personal mindset map.*

Rick is stiring up one department after another with various stories he tells about the future of the company.

Changing a Troubled Future into Something Workable

Rick, cofounder and member of the board, is giving the president of the company headaches. The company has changed. Those exciting days when Rick was needed and critical to the success of the company are gone. It simply isn't the same organization anymore. Those early fragile days when everyone knew and depended on Rick for direction and guidance are no more. Most employees are new and don't even know who he is and don't depend on him for anything. In fact, he is getting in everybody's way. Where in the past he helped, today it is looking more and more like interference.

Getting the map into a clear and accurate statement reflecting Rick's way of meeting his need for approval is the real task. This personal map was governing most of his problem behavior. Seeing his need was easy.

He says, "I'm retiring," to some employees, "I'm in charge of a new division involving you," to other people, and "I'm going back in charge of my old department," to still others in the company. When asked by the president about the conflicting comments, he states emphatically, "I've just got to do something about these vicious rumors!"

With the dramatic growth in the company, things are in turmoil enough even without this key person running amuk and putting things into even more confusion. "Something has to be done," states the company president. So in secret, the company leadership plots and tries various schemes to move Rick out without completely alienating him. But all to no avail. Things are getting worse. Then someone (a change navigator appears on the scene, probably just out of a phone booth from changing his clothes) finally reads what is on Rick's map. He wants attention, to feel important, to be at the center of things, and he is orchestrating to get it. This causes chaos for the organization, but satisfaction and fulfillment for one of its founders. Rick is getting what he wants, but nobody else is. Things are progressively becoming worse.

Then plans begin to hatch in closets where the still-hidden leadership, under the company's president, can find some way to graciously remove Rick. But they now know what would solve the problem: finding something for Rick to do outside the company, meeting his need for importance consistent with the direction dictated by his mindset map. They came up with a solution by putting him in charge of a nonprofit young adult service group. When offered it along with the financial resources to keep his lifestyle from changing (still cheaper than keeping him around), Rick grabbed it. He could charm and lead the youth and be attentive to his needs for being important, also with important bragging rights about the public service he was accomplishing. Besides, the kids needed him and there wasn't anybody else who would take the job. Rick is now doing something worthwhile and out of everyone's corporate hair. All are happy in the new agreement. But without reading Rick's map everyone could still be where they were—stuck.

People Always Follow Their Maps

People behave consistently with their mindset maps. Their choices for what actions to follow are reflected in their maps. Seeing this underlying consistency behind the actions of others allows the navigator to read a person's motivating map. These congruent behavioral patterns can be summarized into a single simple statement. Once you have this statement you can predict what a person will do in a particular situation in the future. Even if only partially accurate, it is much more discernment than most people utilize in interacting with others—which is usually none.

People will often follow their maps with a blind obedience.

A Pattern List—A Discernment Tool

A tool that helps a good deal in the reading of another's map is called *a pattern list.* I first developed it out of frustration when I had a relationship problem with a person at work. I just couldn't figure it out. Racked my brain for weeks about it and just got headaches. Things just weren't working. Everyone said it was, but I could feel that it wasn't working. Something was off, but I couldn't see what. Out of desperation, I simply wrote down on a single reworked piece of paper, over a period of days, what I saw going on, what the other person wanted and talked about in most of his free time. I boiled it down to a list of simple statements of observations. When I finished my list, I even sat down with the other person, went over it and asked him what he thought. It surprised me that with just a few minor modifications, it was accepted as the way he viewed the situation. Then looking at the list (always on only one sheet of paper for a single viewing), the answers jumped off the page at me. What was hidden became obvious. Basically it was that within the actual constraints of the situation and the personalities involved in this partnership, things would never work out well. There were too many conflicting maps. Shortly thereafter everybody was transferred into more effective and agreeable situations.

The wise leader knows what is happening in a group by being aware of what is happening here and now. This is more potent than wandering off into various theories or making complex interpretations of the situation at hand.

Stillness, clarity, and consciousness are more immediate than any number of expeditions into the distant lands of one's mind.

Such expeditions, however stimulating, distract both the leader and the group members from what is actually happening.

By staying present and aware of what is happening, the leader can do less yet achieve more.

John Heider
The Tao of Leadership

Seeing the Obvious

It is surprising how obvious another's maps are once you get the ability to really see, but there is a problem in really seeing. I taught art classes a number of years ago to college students, and the biggest problem I had was getting the art students to see. I had to help them unlearn what they thought they were looking at. They would draw a stylized front view of a person while the model was turned to the side, ignoring what was within their view. They would draw images out of the back of their mind, not what was right in front of their noses, then argue with you that it was what the model actually looked like. I even saw the students draw themselves onto the figure they were sketching. I can still remember the look on one student's face when he realized he was drawing himself onto the beautiful model standing in front of him. Through this entire teaching experience, I was simply trying to get the students to draw what they were seeing, not what they thought they were looking at. I made major headway when I had the students draw from slides that were blurred or upside down, making the familiar things strange, so they couldn't project onto the image what they thought they were looking at and had to draw what was there.

The beginning art students saw and drew what they thought they saw, not what was really there.

The same kind of thing happens when people first try to read another's mindset map. They describe what they think they see, not what is really there. They project themselves and their validations onto the patterns they are supposed to be reading objectively. One thing that helps is to avoid, especially at first, people close to you. The closer you are to a situation or relationship, the harder it is to see. I had a friend around my work for a few days, and he described the company's president in very accurate detail, even predicting his decisions in an approaching merger. Later, I asked him how he was able to do this and he said, "Easy, you are blind and I'm not. You have too much invested into seeing what you want to see, and I couldn't care less."

Learning from Experience

Another story of not seeing what was right in front of my face (I have many of these) was the time I went looking for gold. I was with an old miner and rock hound in the deserts of Utah. I struck it rich, I thought. I found a vein of gold and spent an entire day frantically collecting it. Dreams of wealth filled my head and pushed me on into the late afternoon. Then when I returned to camp and proudly showed him the buckets of hard-earned riches, he proceeded to teach me about what fool's gold was. It was bad enough losing the wealth, but I had to put up with his laughing. Fool's gold is a good term. Don't let inexperience cloud your reactions. Test things out quietly. Play with the process, don't take it too seriously. Then if you're wrong, and you will sometimes be, you won't have to hear the laughter. Besides, it took the fool's gold to learn what real gold looks like.

Reading a Chairman of the Board

For an example, I thought we could pick somebody interesting with a good deal of clout in his company. A person somewhat eccentric and crucial within the organization he commands. Remember that if you want to change an organization, change or help navigate around the key individual. This person's personality saturates the company he leads. In fact, the company may be just an extension of himself.

Here is Roger. All we are really looking for here is his personal map. It is so obvious and so governs everything he does that he provides a good case study. This is only a partial list.

Put on hold any interpretations of the list until you have enough patterns surfacing to indicate an underlying consistency. Also, choose patterns from a diversity of areas. Map reading takes multiple readings from different reference points for accuracy.

The Pattern List

- His corporate office is filled with various awards from organizations and signed photos with positive comments from noted people. No blank space is left open for long without being filled with another award.
- He often makes agreements with interesting new people, but later rescinds the agreement by either forgetting the agreement existed, procrastinating further contact with the person, or letting underlings solve the problem without his involvement.
- He goes from being in one good cause to the next, but never staying very long with one.
- All the ideas he has used in his personal and public life came from someone else.
- He dramatically raises his commanding voice when entering new situations.
- He inserts himself briefly into many situations that have nothing to do with him and ends them with the same comment, "I have such and such important thing to be on to."
- He praises people and values their contribution before he meets them, but later demeans them and their contribution.
- The usual topic of conversation is himself and his next service or contribution.
- He talks of a person being "his closest friend," but over a few years time the relationships are consistently severed or become distant.
- He often seen in situations where he is at the center.
- He hires or surrounds himself with famous people who contribute only their name to the situation.
- He consistently steps in to save his extended family from various and chronic problems they are having.
- He often mentions or alludes to the mistreatment his family received from a certain high social circle that they were once in.
- His mother is brought to all social situations where he is viewed as exemplary in some way or another.
- He never refutes when others give him sole authorship for things he didn't do and things he worked on with others.

As leader and chief icon for the company his choices over the years, big ones and thousands of little seemingly inconsequential ones, have directed his company to both its successes and its failures to the present day. I will call him Roger, and he is the corporate CEO to one the fastest- rising companies in America. Here is the partial pattern list and map reading on these two pages about Roger:

Consistencies

His Personal Mindset Map

Courses of Action for the Navigator

He feeds on the notoriety of important people. When he connects with one and uses them, he moves on to another. Must make continual new associations to keep this going.

Must have an approving audience to show his important contributions to. Has some deep need for constant and continual approval.

Seems driven by the fix of the present need for approval. Past and anticipated events are brought up in the present for that approval.

Family seems the only stable association in his life, though he has a lot of superficial associations with important people in various occupations that are stated as long-term.

> **I'm only important when I'm seen in important situations with important people.**
>
> Being Valued

This is an educated guess, but I think we are in the area of some accuracy.

If you are going to navigate through Roger's world, you are going to have to face his map, with its immense need for outside approval. Here are some possibilities:

• Raising your own status within his eyes is important, but avoid close contact that will automatically diminish your value. Important people and approval-gaining situations have a shelf life with Roger.

• Connecting with his family may help. They are stable within his world.

• Be a source for new ideas he can use to gain new approval.

• Provide Roger with a way to gain more exposure to the public eye and notice from important people.

• Trying to change this mindset map of Rogers is useless now. Too many things are giving his map validation. Within his world the map works to a point, even though it isn't lasting. If only you could find a way to give Roger eternal approval!

The Change Navigator must decide what his or her purpose in interacting with Roger is, what he or she wants to accomplish and, from the map readings, develop a strategy to navigate through Roger's world.

Warning: Keep a wary eye on yourself and face the fact that your map can color all you see. Stalk yourself and your maps to see that you're are not forcing evidence onto the map that you want to be true rather than what you really see motivating them. I believe total objectivity is an illusion, but awareness of your own coloring can help you see things much more clearly.

Prime Indicators

People behave all the time. That is what they naturally do. If you had to follow them around trying to read what they have written on their maps, you could go nuts, but rest easy. All you really need to look for are a few things exhibiting the underlying consistency of their most important map. **Everything around a person tends to manifest his or** her personal mindset map, but only a few prime indicators need to be read by a navigator in order to read with clarity this motivating map.

Here are some prime indicators:
- **Watch** for impression management of a certain *image* people want to be seen as.
- **Look** for the *opposite* of some point that they keep pushing. Listen for *free information* (wasn't asked for or called for within the setting).
- **Look** at their *key relationships* and how they keep confirming or negating some point.
- **See** their *orchestrations* to cause others to respond emotionally in a set way.
- **Listen** for all *validating statements*.
- **Look** for the *extreme states* when they are the most happy or most depressed.

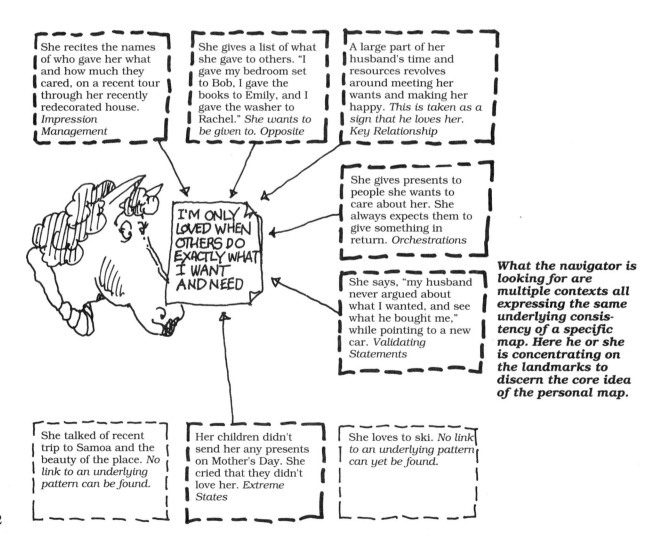

She recites the names of who gave her what and how much they cared, on a recent tour through her recently redecorated house. *Impression Management*

She gives a list of what she gave to others. "I gave my bedroom set to Bob, I gave the books to Emily, and I gave the washer to Rachel." *She wants to be given to. Opposite*

A large part of her husband's time and resources revolves around meeting her wants and making her happy. *This is taken as a sign that he loves her. Key Relationship*

She gives presents to people she wants to care about her. She always expects them to give something in return. *Orchestrations*

I'M ONLY LOVED WHEN OTHERS DO EXACTLY WHAT I WANT AND NEED

She says, "my husband never argued about what I wanted, and see what he bought me," while pointing to a new car. *Validating Statements*

She talked of recent trip to Samoa and the beauty of the place. *No link to an underlying pattern can be found.*

Her children didn't send her any presents on Mother's Day. She cried that they didn't love her. *Extreme States*

She loves to ski. *No link to an underlying pattern can yet be found.*

What the navigator is looking for are multiple contexts all expressing the same underlying consistency of a specific map. Here he or she is concentrating on the landmarks to discern the core idea of the personal map.

A person's most important map will be expressed throughout all the choices he or she makes.

The Outward Manifestations of the Inside Map

You don't need to read everything a person does to discern what directs his or her motivations. Only those indicators that exhibit the most important map are important to be read. With mindset maps there are prime indicators or certain consistent behaviors that stand out. These are the outward manifestations in varying situations of the same internal map. The most important map is usually his or her personal mindset map. Everything is often routed through this single map, which is typically driven by deep and unmet needs. These needs find expression and seek fulfillment throughout the actions and choices of daily life, telegraphing through a framework of consistency what the underlying map is. I call these consistent expressions of this map the *Prime Indicators,* and they'll give you the map you're trying to find as a doorway to reaching and affecting those you must deal with. Here are the most common prime indicators to read:

Watch for impression management of a certain *image* the person wants to convey. Impression management is the deliberate manipulation of information for the purpose of maintaining of a specific desired image. Here are some examples:

- Johnson & Johnson's openness to the public and fast reaction after the Tylenol capsules were poisoned, causing death. Making it public knowledge that they were pulling the medication off the shelves nationwide and rapidly developing an alternative (caplets and sealed containers) for protection against this ever happening again. (Image of a responsible and caring company.)

- Ryan saying to all the members of the team in Thursday's practice, "*I don't think I'll be able to play well against them on Saturday because I've been ill for weeks. I may not even be able to play. With my age and this illness, maybe I should quit.*" (Image of uncontrollable events making him quit the team.)

- "*Dad, remember when you said you would always love me no matter what I did? Remember those bad things you said about what the neighbors did, and remember their large patio window, and that you thought I was a good ball player . . .?*"

Look for the *opposite* of some point that they keep pushing.

Look for their map to be the opposite of what they keep talking about.

Since people seek satisfaction of their needs, what is most on their mind is the fulfillment of some need and the map directing how the need is to be filled. People push some idea to attain it. If they had already achieved it, it would no longer be on their mind. You don't talk of eating food if you are stuffed. You don't talk of being safe if you are. You are driven on some need by the lack of it.

- Courtney's constant talk of women's power and rights. Her dislike of men and men as the reasons for the problems women have. (Her own powerlessness, abuse as a child.)

- Comments from Shane on how unprofessional and incompetent the other salesmen in the office are. (Worried about his own competence.)

• Sandy's blaming other women in the neighborhood for not staying home and being with their children. (She envies them and wants out.)

Listen for *free information* (wasn't asked for or called for within the setting). The information they just give out when the situation doesn't call for them to say it, particularly at odd or inopportune times, indicates a map guiding them toward meeting some need that is pressing on their mind.

• *"Elaine brought up three times in the committee meeting on the corporate legal action, her appointment to the national chairmanship of her association."* (Her image of importance.)

• During a phone call from Alice trying to find out about Allen's position on the report, she keeps mentioning her position. (Her fear of not being accepted by the others in her department.)

• At a solemn funeral you expect certain things: tears, black, sadness, recollections, heads down, a quiet pace, etc. At the funeral, Darnel, the deceased person's son, talks on and on about his new car, all the funeral expenses not being covered by the insurance, and the disposition of his father's property. (His concern for his financial position and status.)

Look at their *key relationships* and how they keep confirming or negating some point. The most important area of people's lives, where they seek confirmation for their personal map, is in their major relationships. Our well being and personal definition seems to depend on the confirming actions of others. If you want to read their map, see the validating done within their relationships.

Their most important relationhip, whether it is with a person, an animal, their job, their past history, etc., is where you can read their maps the easiest.

• Bob's wife constantly measuring him against her higher standards and Bob's constantly trying to match those standards for a higher social and intellectual status. (She feels superior to her husband, and he feels inferior to her.)

• Mathew's comments at lunch on how beautiful his wife is compared with everyone else and that he couldn't stand to be married to woman like Mary with her overweight problem. He also mentions how he is a gourmet cook, his new Lexus and his job with a prestigious position and company, and all this with her supporting comments. (Image of being and having just the special right things makes him right.)

• Will's statement about his job: "There is always a better way and I'm always searching for it. Any new improvements are immediately instigated into my program. It is the best I've found." (Superiority of method equals superiority of self.)

See their *orchestrations* to cause others to respond emotionally in a set way. Where their effort goes is where their map is. People will deliberately seek confirmation of what is on their map by manipulating situations to achieve it, often pulling enormous resources to elicit the desired response.

People spend their resources of time, effort, money, knowledge, skills, etc., trying to align their world to their map.

• He divorced his wife and married his assistant. Then under a cloud of accusations of corporate and personal impropriety, both of them maneuvered the company into a corporate takeover costing millions of dollars. (They wanted to be seen as a competent team, not lovers.)

Don't get caught in the retoric.

"It is precisely because we have been advocating co-existence that we have shed so much blood."
Yasir Arafat

"Let me make it perfectly clear."
Richard Nixon

- *"Watch him. Every time anyone in the family asks Jerry how he is doing, he goes through the same procedure. He first slumps his shoulders, then bows his head, then he starts to cry about how much he loved her and misses her, and finally he firmly states, now with head held high, that he is doing all he can for the kids."* (He wanted to be seen as the innocent victim doing all he possibly could.)

- *"Before the final meeting on Tuesday, Jack had gone to each of their offices and even to Mike's home and lobbied for his position. He even called and pressured Noel while he was on his vacation. It worked! On Tuesday, with all this support, he creamed Diana's opposing position. He gloated after at lunch about his extremely effective strategy and skill."* (The most skillful and cunning, thus most competent.)

Listen for all *validating statements*. People will bring up the support they seek—they will say it. You can hear what they want their map to be. All validating statements reflect their most important map and how it causes them to see their world.

- Karen has said these same things through all the years I've known her: *"I'm at a loss. I try and try and try, but he still continues his rotten behavior. He never appreciates what I've done for him. I've done all I can do."* (Another martyr—there are a great many of them out there.)

- Validating statements by an acquaintance in just one 20 minute phone call, none of them asked for: *"If that was me, I would have stood up for my principles." "I feel people are in the wrong to do it the way you did." "A person should stand for something over his own selfishness." "I have never weakened my position." "Don't you have more courage than that?" "People should stand for something."* (I'm superior to you because of my complete adherence to higher principles.)

Look for the *extreme states* when they are the most happy or the most depressed. When a need has been reached the way their map said it was supposed to, or totally rejected by situations completely voiding their map, then you have a clearer view of the underlying map. Total rejection or complete acceptance of a map provides you with the contrasting extremes for a sharper image of their map.

- After being fired, Sherman went to all the people in the office and tried to rally them into angry defiance against his supervisor's reasoning. (Having trouble with his value as a person was linked to his job.)

- His face lights up when he talks of the award, and he goes into in-depth detail at any hint you might be interested. (Recognition is very important.)

- She couldn't stop talking about meeting this guy and how neat he was and on and on. (May depend on a personal relationship for value.)

A Good Question

A good question to ask after reading some *prime indicators* is, "What basic need does this action or behavior seem aimed at fulfilling?" And, "What do they believe will get this need satisfied for them?" You are looking for a thread of consistency between what you have observed as their need linked to how they are trying to fill it. Their need is usually very easy to see, and once you have discovered how they plan on meeting that need, you have got their personal map.

85

Map Predicting

The effectiveness of a navigator's map reading is determined by the read map's accuracy in predicting the future responses of its owner. A read map is only as good as its predictability. This one factor separates the masters from the amateurs. The read map is used to discern how another will react in future situations. The future is where there is any real use for reading the person's map in the first place. If the map isn't accurate in determining future responses, it is useless in navigating change.

Here is Phil's read map, followed by guesses of what he will do in future situations, and finally what really happened. All this is an exercise to check out the accuracy of how his map was read:

2. Guess the Response
Predict what he or she would do in a particular situation that is about to happen.

3. Compare the Actuality with the Prediction
Match what you thought would happen with what reallly did. How close did you come?

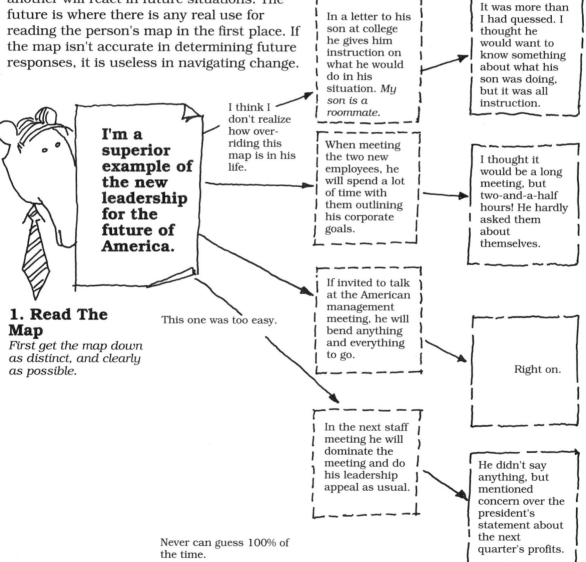

1. Read The Map
First get the map down as distinct, and clearly as possible.

I'm a superior example of the new leadership for the future of America.

I think I don't realize how over-riding this map is in his life.

In a letter to his son at college he gives him instruction on what he would do in his situation. *My son is a roommate.*

It was more than I had quessed. I thought he would want to know something about what his son was doing, but it was all instruction.

When meeting the two new employees, he will spend a lot of time with them outlining his corporate goals.

I thought it would be a long meeting, but two-and-a-half hours! He hardly asked them about themselves.

This one was too easy.

If invited to talk at the American management meeting, he will bend anything and everything to go.

Right on.

In the next staff meeting he will dominate the meeting and do his leadership appeal as usual.

He didn't say anything, but mentioned concern over the president's statement about the next quarter's profits.

Never can guess 100% of the time.

Hitting It Right On and Missing It by a Mile

What follow are a few examples of my predicting abilities:

- I was involved with a museum project in Chicago. I was part of a large team of experts drawn from all over the country to work on expanding a museum. Each of these people were considered by the person directing the project to be the top within their separate fields. What I read, though, was that this entire project would never go anywhere and wasn't meant to. It was simply an orchestration by an outside consultant in charge of the project to feed his need for power and validation under the excuse of helping the museum. He overpowered the director with extravagant talk of joint superhuman achievement, but his needs were larger than their budget. I read it was going nowhere, which it did, and I got out. This wasn't so complicated to read; it's a common occurrence.

- There is one predicting approach that is simple and effective. You read what a person wants to achieve in validation of an image of him or herself, then provide a way to accomplish it for an exchange of what you want. A corporate president wanted to become an expert in a particular area. I studied the area and provided a way to accomplish it. He determined the direction with his need for a certain validation; I simply helped create the vehicle to get there. Hundreds of thousand of dollars later, he got his objective and I got the financial reward.

With predicting you may have a few problems or a few rewards.

- I used to live in a relatively rich area (we called it Yuppie Acres) where all the home owners took great pride in their yards. Each one tried to outdo his or her neighbor in landscaping. But there was a problem by the name of Prince, one neighbor's dog. He was always digging up things and leaving presents for people to step in. This practice of Prince's got to the point of heated arguments. It didn't take much brilliance to read the maps and the future here—escalation until we had yuppie fights with "your lawyer talking to my lawyer." Being raised on a farm, I knew how to get out of all this. I knew dogs marked their territory with their urine. Fences and property rights don't mean anything to a dog. So I waited until my wife and kids left (the explanation wasn't worth it) and filled a jar. I then went outside and marked my yard, and Prince obeyed. Then one day one of the arguing neighbors came over as I was watering my yard, and with a searching question, wondered why Prince and his doings never ventured onto my yard. Like an idiot, I told him. It took months to calm down the talk of a neighborhood pervert.

Run Some Map Predicting Experiments of Your Own

The accuracy of reading another's map is in how closely predictions taken from them match the actuality. An exercise that sharpens this skill is to make predictions of people's responses in specific future situations. Predict from people's maps you think you have accurately read. Try guessing their reactions to things you can see coming. For example, a meeting will happen tomorrow to present concepts for a new product (predicting things you are not directly involved in is a lot easier). The person whoes map you've read will be there. Predict their reactions in the meeting. Here's another example: Take a person whose map you think you have accurately read and introduce them to someone you know. Guess what their reaction will be to the new person. Write these predictions down beforehand (nobody else needs to see them) and date it (we do a lot of fudging on things like this). Stay out of validating yourself on these predictions; it cripples the whole process. More on this later.

A poor navigator loses his map, reads it upside-down or never checks its accuracy.

Discernment Blocks

Discernment is the art of seeing things as they really are. It is penetrating deeper than the obvious and superficial surface of things, grasping and comprehending what lies hidden underneath. It is going beyond the rhetorical barrage and theatrical machinations of daily life into what is actually running things.

To learn how to really see it is more a matter of getting rid of some preconceived ideas than learning anything new. There are three things we most need to remove from ourselves to fully discern the reading of maps.

The first is *self-validation* with its constant need for achieving value from outside ourselves. Next is getting caught into someone's map, *contaminated* by the view through another's eyes and not our own. And finally is the fear of accepting what we see. The truth always extracts a price we may not be willing to pay. The three in more detail:

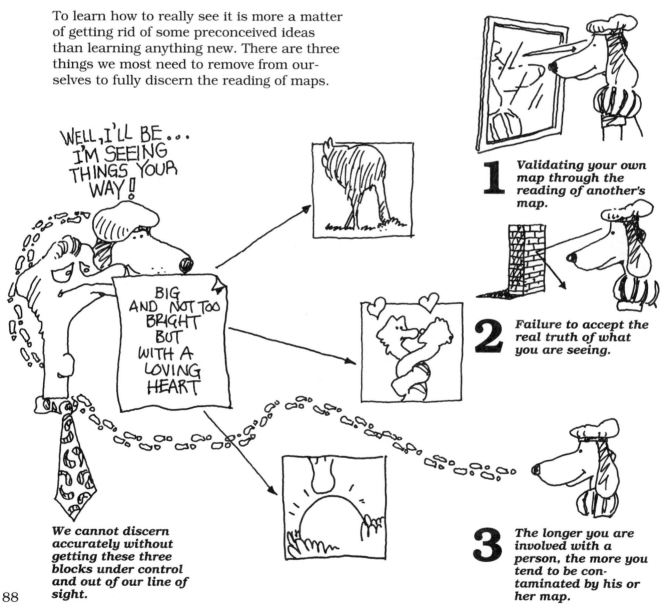

1 *Validating your own map through the reading of another's map.*

2 *Failure to accept the real truth of what you are seeing.*

3 *The longer you are involved with a person, the more you tend to be contaminated by his or her map.*

We cannot discern accurately without getting these three blocks under control and out of our line of sight.

Three Blocks to Seeing Things as They Really Are

For a change navigator to clearly read someone's reality and to understand how they will react to future changes, they must remove anything blinding their discernment. These perceptual blocks can cause navigators to sail blindly into waters thinking they have charted the route, but they are actually directing their ships into dangerous shoals. A blind navigator is as useless, as an unmagnetized compass. To follow them anywhere is at the least, useless and at the most, deadly. Here are blocks to seeing, that if dealt with can get the navigator's eyes open, clear and reading maps accurately:

1. Validating your own map through the situation you are trying to discern. Looking for evidence to support our own personal map while trying to read another's mindset map blinds us to reading their maps accurately. *Change Navigators* must be able to put their own maps and the validation that they crave on the shelf before they can read someone else's map. *You just can't see clearly another's map while validating your own.* Obsessed with validating their own maps, navigators will end up only viewing their vain reflections. They will construe and intertwine someone else's life into validating their own, creating a very warped image onto which they take their measurements and plot their course in interacting with others. Because of this, the people the navigators are reading are seen as dumber than they, more in error than they are, or lesser or higher beings than the navigators are. Because their egos so saturate their map reading an absurd comparing process creates asinine conclusions inferred from interpreting these maps.

Validating your own map through the reading of others, causes you only to map your own reflection.

I have found that for this validation not to happen, it takes constant effort and continual vigilance. The old ego, once removed, will keep sneaking back and thwarting any accurate perception, especially an ego with a abundance of hubris. The fact that this is always the case, accepting that it will happen again and again, and constantly guarding against it, is the biggest deterrent to self-validation tainting the maps. To illustrate, take the following story:

You can loose your ego in the Northwest Territories, bury it in the backyard of a home in Talleshasse, or shoot it to the back side of the moon, but it will always sneak back and crawl up onto your face and block your clear reading of maps. Constantly fumigate against it.

In the late 50s, General Motors dominated the car industry. Ford was losing customers as the consumers upgraded to more expensive cars. Unlike General Motors, Ford had a void in its line of cars. The small Fords competed with Chevrolet, and the Lincoln competed with the Cadillac; however, Ford had no competitor with the Oldsmobile. So, Ford created the Edsel (named after Henry Ford's son). It was a creation behind closed doors within the aloof offices of top management—a car more for validating the name and power of the Ford family than providing something the customer actually wanted. The customer was supposed to want the car because the company leadership wanted the car. The Edsel debued and bombed in 1958.

On the other hand, also in the late 50s, American Motors, under George Romney, saw a niche in the marketplace that neither Ford nor General Motors was selling to. He saw a need for a small, economical and dependable car. He saw what the customer really wanted. While Detroit was caught in a spasm of bigger is better, with longer hoods, huge fenders

89

and fins, American Motors created the Rambler. In the recession year of 1958, its sales increased dramatically while the sales of other companies dropped. One company read the customer maps and acted on the predictions while another read their own reflection.

Getting contaminated by another's map. The longer you are involved with people, the more you tend to be influenced by how they see the world. You tend to look at the world using their map and not yours, viewing things through their eyes and not your own. Navigators' own discernment will naturally be affected by others' when they have to work closely with them. Over time, through close association, navigators lose their ability to see clearly from the outside vantage point.

It is like there is a clock ticking, and eventually you will be contaminated in your perception as you work with others. The closer you associate, the faster the clock ticks until you can't see clearly. Removing yourself from the situation for a time, asking for help from an unbiased observer, and giving yourself a time limit when working with others are all methods to cope with this tendency. Again, some illustrations:

The longer you are involved with a person, the more you tend to be contaminated by his or her map.

A clock is always ticking in any relationship until you will be contaminated.

Accepting another's map as your own automatically blinds you in ever clearly reading his or her map.

• A company originally took two days to do the proposal which led to their breadwinner product. As the company grew, developing alternative products took longer and longer to create, until finally all product development came to a halt and the department they had set up for this very purpose was disbanded. No new products have been put into the marketplace since then. The maps of all involved were so blinded by the success of the first proposal that no new products were ever really considered.

• Our doctor has a definite rule. He will not deliver his own baby, but lets another doctor do it. He is very qualified, even more so than the doctors his wife uses. He once tried, but got so emotionally involved with his wife and child in a very dangerous delivery (another doctor helped him out of it), that he will not do it anymore.

The fear of accepting the truth of what we have discerned. The truth demands a price many of us fail to pay. What we want, what we hope for, what we are seeking, and the desire to have things be a set way, all stop us from really seeing. The truth can often be a hard taskmaster asking us to accept things we have never wanted to, whipping deep into preconceived notions and wished-for dreams. We may have to stop reading some people's or institution's maps and decide that it isn't worth the pain of facing what we'll find. Failure to accept things as they really are, I have found, is the biggest barrier to being an effective *Change Navigator.*

Something that has kept me going all these years, while I was often failing and picking myself up and trying again and again, are some questions. The first is, what else have I really got than the truth? It is always an approximation, but better that than all the lies. Better to build on a solid base of things as they really are than on the shifting foundation of self-delusion. And the last question: The ancient navigators sailed in little wooden ships, pushing the edge of their world, and they found a new one. Why can't I? As always, more examples:

• In the 1930s, the French put millions of dollars in the Maginot Line. The line was a long fortified embankment facing the German border. It was designed to stop Germany's direct invasion of France. Yet, in both previous wars, Germany had gone north through Belgium into France. In the second World War, Germany flanked the Maginot line in a matter of hours. One young Frenchman by the name of Charles de Gaulle had predicted Germany would do so. He saw what was always there while the leadership didn't.

• During America's involvement in the Vietnam War, Ho Chi Minh, the leader of North Vietnam, is reported to have predicted America's eventual withdrawal from the conflict. He said the Americans were an impatient people unaware of the Asians' willingness to fight 30 years, if necessary, in order to reunite their country. He waited and trusted his perceptions for 30 years. How long could we?

A few words of Scott Peck's that talk about maps and truth better than I could:

Failure to accept the real truth of what you are seeing makes you lose the power you might have had.

". . . must continually be employed if our lives are to be healthy and our spirits are to grow, is dedication to the truth. Superficially, this should be obvious. For truth is reality. That which is false is unreal. The more clearly we see the reality of the world, the better equipped we are to deal with the world. The less clearly we see the reality of the world—the more our minds are befuddled by falsehood, misperceptions and illusions—the less able we will be to determine correct courses of action and make wise decisions. Our view of reality is like a map with which to negotiate the terrain of life. If the map is true and accurate, we will generally know where we are, and if we have decided where we want to go, we will generally know how to get there. If the map is false and inaccurate, we generally will be lost.

"While this is obvious, it is something that most people to a greater or lesser degree choose to ignore. They ignore it because our route to reality is not easy. First of all, we are not born with maps; we have to make them, and the making requires effort. The more effort we make to appreciate and perceive reality, the larger and more accurate our maps will be. But many do not want to make this effort. Some stop making it by the end of adolescence. Their maps are small and sketchy, their views of the world narrow and misleading. By the end of middle age most people have given up the effort. They feel certain their maps are correct . . . and they are no longer interested in new information. It is as if they are tired. Only a relative and fortunate few continue until the moment of death exploring the mystery of reality, ever enlarging and refining and redefining their understanding of the world and what is true."

M. Scott Peck
A Road Less Traveled

In refusing to accept the truth for what it is we deny the power contained within it.

Power Centers

If you want to change an organization, then select those people within the organization having power and change them. Affect them, affect the organization. Change them, the institution changes.

But don't get the wrong idea that the typical organization chart reflects anything to do with the real power. Statements like the charts, high-sounding goals, showpiece leadership and impressive titles are just well-intended fantasies or deliberate camouflage. They seldom, if ever, show the real power and the real motives. The real power is in the individuals and their connections with each other that can impose their individual maps on the group. If the group sees by a certain map that it is controlled by the owner of that map, there is where the real power is.

The public image of the institution presented to society and its members is often only a surface covering. This image can keep the public from seeing what the organization is really about and who is actually in charge.[14]

The people who can impose their own map on the group are where the real power is. They often form into a network to do this, within the institution. Each node of the network is a power center. These centers may be diffuse or coalesce around a few or a single person.

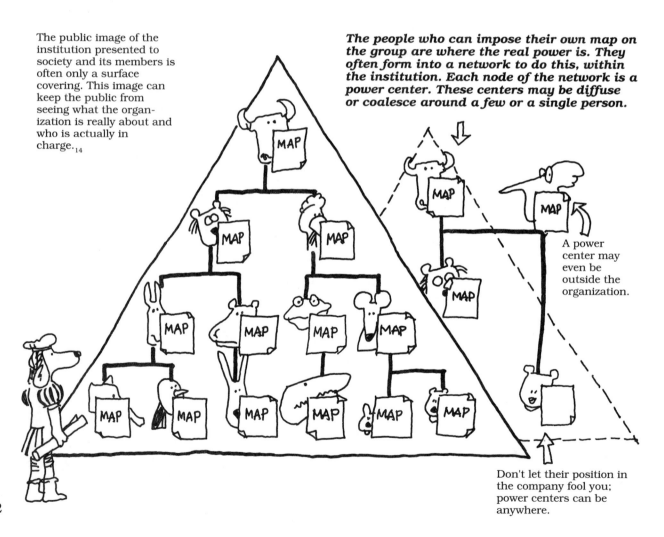

A power center may even be outside the organization.

Don't let their position in the company fool you; power centers can be anywhere.

Moving a Group into Accepting a New Map

An organization or institution doesn't exist independently of its people, but collectively, organizations do seem to have a single persona. Though it functions at a much cruder level than an individual's would, it often perceives and thinks in ways any rational individual would find absurd and even wrong (institutions can be childish, even retarded, and sometimes psychotic). But the problem is when individual members of any organization acquiesce their own maps and perceptions to the simplistic and single-minded map of the whole (group thinking). Some examples:

An organization can function like an individual, but in a cruder and less intelligent way.

- Hitler and a political group called the Nazi Party took control over a tired nation and tried imposing a 1,000-year third rein for an Aryan nation on the world. 13 years later, 55 million souls had died in the process. Hitler never killed a single one of them. The institution that bought his map did.

- When asked why he could tell them about the present state of their organization in such detail without knowing anything about it but a simple description, a management consultant said the following, *"It's easy; organizations naturally tend to lose the dynamics of the beginning, grow old and, with increasing age, die. At each stage of growth in an organization, as with an individual, there are set stages, from the exuberance and creativity of youth, into the growth and development of maturity and finally into the rigidity and decay of old age, ending in death."*

- Comments from a friend who is now a U.S. Senator: "In my dealings with Washington it is the civil servants and lobbyists who rule. They have the power of tenure, knowledge and money. The presidents and congress come and go. The band plays, the slogans are declared and business continues on in the direction it did before. The real power brokers play the real game underneath it all. They know the game, know how to play it, know the players, and are around a long time to play. They function with one thought in mind—maintaining their turf."

- Near where I live is a 19th-century grave of a man hung by a town. They were so upset by his crime and the legal system not dealing with him in the way they thought it should, that they simply banded together and executed him at the end of a rope. I don't think any one of these people involved would have done the hanging individually, but collectively they did.

Group thinking isn't very intelligent. Institutions are naturally retarded and slow to adapt by themselves and often never do. To change a group map in mass takes a committed group with a map willing to devote the time and effort to impose their map onto the other group. A political campaign or a media blitz, for example. And you are only a single navigator.

I believe our society's institutions are increasingly becoming more and more polarized making them harder and harder to change. A kind of advanced rigor mortis is filling our corporate and institutional halls. Collectively they are unwilling and unable to adapt to change. They seem frozen into only the robot-like responses of the past, as rapid change overpowers many of them. Today, I see the most effective way to cause change within an organization or institution is to concentrate your effort as a *Change Navigator* only on the

OK WHEN
STABLE

CRUMBLES
WHEN NOT

*Organizations may
have maps so
unchangeable and rigid
that the least movement
can bring them down.
During times of change
they collapse in a heap
with a little shaking,
like being in a building
not designed to
withstand an
earthquake.*

key people within it. If you can change the maps of these *Power
Centers*, or the key people with power enough to move the map of
an organization, you can change the larger group. If you can't do
that, the organization will probably not change; the momentum of
the status quo is just too strong a current for one navigator to sail
against.

Change Their Maps and Everthing Else Follows

I have found trying to change these institutions, that are rampant
with this group thinking, in any kind of straightforward manner
useless, and if the organization is threatened by any of the alternatives presented, it can be downright dangerous. You change an
organization by changing the power structure—the institution's
leadership. Change the leadership, and the organization will
change. But it has to be the real leadership, with the real power. A
change navigator should be *selective* in who he or she is reading
and is trying to affect, only choosing the persons linked to the lines
of power within an organization if he wants to change the institution. This power network seldom matches the clean and neat
organizational charts companies and institutions are so eager to
create. Power is much more dynamic and subtle than that.

**I have found that the biggest indicator of power within a
company is the individuals who are able to impose their own
maps onto the group's map.** Any person who can impose his or
her own map onto the group's map, giving the organization the
same view of the world as he or she has, has real power.

Inside institutions, the individuals imposing their own maps on the
organization's form into a network of like-minded people with these
common aims: to maintain their unified map, to further its allegiance and to apply its instructions to the combined membership
of the group; each node of this network is a power center. These
centers may be diffuse or coalesce around a few people or a single
person. Trace these lines in the organizational structure and you've
got the power centers. Remember, these real lines of power never
follow the organizational charts every large group has framed in
their conference rooms and on their annual reports. If you can
affect these linked individual maps, the entire organization map
will follow. A simple story to illustrate:

*When herding animals,
you have two ways to
do it: first, the hard
way, forcing them all to
move in the direction
you want; second, the
easier way, finding the
lead animal and moving
just it, and the herd will
follow.*

In one little company the president had me do a profile of their customers (read their maps). These customer maps were extremely consistent,
and any time you have this kind of group consistency, you have an
opportunity. This company was third in their market and wanted to
expand. I developed a change in how they viewed themselves towards
better meeting the expectations of their customers.

Their customer clearly wanted the company's products packaged for
them into easy-to-use modules. This was more costly than letting the
customers choose and assemble the products for themselves, but the

maps I was reading were very consistent and they were more than willing to pay for this new packaging. I talked the president into a test with one trial product, and the results were all he needed. This company now dominates the markets, and over 80% of their sales are these new modules. Seeing their customers in a new light created a changed company map that made it much more responsive and effective with those customers.

About Changing Organizations

What follow are some factors that should be considered when attempting to cause change within any institution:

• The first factor is that the best vehicle for orchestrating validation of an individual's map is usually an organization with an idealized map, especially an organization built on some public virtue. It protects the individual from contradiction. To attack him or her is to attack the virtue because, "I'm not doing this for me, it is for God, country, motherhood, garbage pick-up, and educating your children." So, beware of power centers who are in the organization because it provides excellent defense and is a vehicle for validating fragile personal maps. Change to these people is an enemy.

• Another factor is that the more absolute and perfect the leadership's *(Power Centers)* view of the world through their map, the more rigid and unadaptable the institution. Any request for change is greeted with the reply, "This is perfect, and who are you to question things?" When an institution has this idea and things are not working out perfectly or even getting worse, but things should be perfect according to the map, then the only rational response is that someone must be messing things up. So the cry goes out, "Get a rope and find him!" Any navigator asking questions and messing around while perfection is cracking and becoming imperfect should lie low for awhile unless he desires to be a scapegoat for some idealizing fanatics wanting revenge and an excuse. Martyrs can cause change, but they tend to not be around to enjoy it.

• Still another factor to consider is that most organizational maps are metaphorical in their form. This kind of map has all the people in the institution collectively seeing themselves as a defending army, a winning football team, a missionary, a machine, a savior, an assembly line, an artist, a home or a shining example, etc. This metaphorical map is a central icon providing the glue that holds its employees or members together. It may be the main framework from which all the other subordinate maps are linked; change it and everything else must change.

Change the metaphor used in their group map, and how everyone jointly views things will change too. When this happens, their collective response will also be different.

If you can get the people (the Power Centers) to change this central metaphor into one more conducive to the needed changes, then the entire organization may move into the future with more strength. I worked with a company that changed its map from one of a family to one of a provisioner. Also, I know of an institution that changed its map from one of a machine to one of an armorer of warriors for an approaching battle. The change in viewpoint and response in both cases was very dramatic. But you need someone accepted in the institution who can help you drive this new metaphor into the organization's map with unflappable resolve.

• And the last factor is, if history is any indication, successful leaders with power, who will change themselves and will exert the energy necessary to redirect the momentum of their organizations, are very rare, even when they see change as critical. But leaders who are unsuccessful and without complete power in changing the direction of their organization will sometimes listen. It was struggling Spain that listened to Columbus, not Italy, his home, or the other powerful nations of Europe.

The Right Map

Inside   Outside

I'M RIGHT about being a very good person and that everyone likes and approves of me.

I'll be secure when I find another person who I can trust to take care of me.

APP

The following map is so common that navigators should continually be aware of it when reading anybody's map. It stands in the way of working directly and openly with most people, dominating the majority of situations and relationships the navigator is trying to steer through.

A superior map may replace an inferior map except when a person is presenting an idealized *Right Map* for outside validation to contradict and hide the real map inside. Individuals often fuse with their personal mindset maps, transforming their maps into themselves. When their map is found wrong, incomplete and not enough (maps always are, eventually), these map's owners also become these things. Then people, ashamed of these flaws that are now their own, cover their maps over with idealized maps which have all the things they think they lack. They then proceeds to manipulate control over events and people to validate these idealized maps, shielding the inside maps from any outside exposure which would prove that they are wrong and flawed. Deep changes are now denied. Any attempts to update these maps automatically expose the people to invalidation of themselves. The navigator must read this common facade of "Right Maps," covering the actual maps being followed, in order to learn to navigate effectively.

The **Inside Map** is mistakenly confused with the person and is deliberately hidden from view. To expose this map, which they really believe is wrong to have, is to expose themselves as wrong.

The **"Right Map"** is presented for outside acceptance because it is not flawed, is enough, and is the right map to have. Since this map is also confused with its owner, both the map and the person are considered having the same qualities.

Both these maps, the flawed one actually being followed and the ideal one that they are trying to convince everyone that they are using, fuse with the owner's personality. The maps and the map's creator are considered to be one and the same.

The Most Common Map

The following map is the biggest problem there is to change, making life very complicated for the navigator. When it isn't there, things are simple and direct and you worry about communication and comprehension problems. But when this map is there, you worry about strategy and secrecy problems. Without this map you can plot a course in roughly a straight line, but if this map is present, your route often looks like a course through a convoluted maze.

Not Being Able to Separate the People From Their Maps

People, for whatever reason, often combine their personal mindset maps with themselves. They and their map become one and the same. They see no differentiation between the map and who they really are. The arrow on the map, pointing out in bold fashion, you are here, has been interpreted as fact. They've confused the map with themselves. This fusing the two together freezes the map where it is, and they lose the power that comes from following a constantly updated and more accurate map. The person is then locked into the powerlessness of an obsolete map, following its errors into whatever misadventure awaits. Like a pilot trying to use a 16th-century map and getting lost. It is an absurd idea, but a typical tendency of the vast majority including, when there is a full moon, myself.

Creating Two Maps, With the Ideal Map Concealing the Actual Map Being Used

Because the map is now inseparable from its owner, when it is discovered that the map isn't perfect, right, or enough to completely know the territory (no map ever is), its owner will have the same flaws. He or she will now be imperfect, wrong, not enough, not OK, invalid, mistaken, corrupted, in error, etc. When this happens, an outside ideal map, opposite from the flawed map, is created. It is *"The Right Map"* and it is *supposed* to take the place of the incomplete map. But the first map doesn't disappear; it is just hidden underneath. People also confuse themselves with this idealized perfect map. With the adoption of this "right map" begins two processes: First, everything and anything is measured against this ideal map. And secondly, because it is covering up the actual but disgusting (ashamed of it as themselves) map underneath, there begins a search for outside validation that this ideal "Right Map" is the only true and correct map there is. To illustrate these two maps:

This typical map provides the cover-up for a deep feeling of "wrongness" that many people have. This map is promoted by them as the central reference point by which all their relationships are defined. This defining is with all relationships, whether they be with people, things, money, ideas, places, time, etc.

Remember, RIGHT means different things to different folks:

Right to a martyr may mean getting burned tied to the stake.

Right to a masochist may mean getting hurt.

Right to someone superior may mean having people fawn all over them.

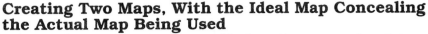

• My wife had a roommate when she lived in Los Angeles who gave her constant instructions until she could take it no longer and moved: *"You should have cleaned the kitchen like you found it. I had just cleaned it. You never introduce me to him. If I were you, I would. You didn't cook that right, the way we have it at home. You ought to be more considerate. I respect your things. You could have called and told me you would be late. You should have told me you were going."* The last my wife heard of her was a letter commenting on how much she missed her best friend. Possibly a disguise of superiority was hiding real loneliness.

Many of our maps are often passed down from generation to generation with errors and all.

• A funny reply from a colleague when asked what happened to a person we both know: *"He talked a good deal about integrity right up until he was arrested for embezzling."*

• A number of years ago we had a neighborhood kid steal some stuff. No police were involved, but when it was brought to his mom's attention, she said, *"My son would never do such a thing! How dare you even insinuate!"* I knew it was her son because I saw him, but nevertheless the things stolen mysteriously ended up put back. Then a few days later one of my little kids was over at their house (guess she forgot who the child belonged to) when his mother was chewing out her kid for the stealing. Two maps: the sanitary, ideal public one and then the real one.

• The daughter of a mother who has an obviously favorite child (and it isn't her) recently said the following: *"I can't understand why mother kept saying the house my brother was renting was so terribly awful for him before he moved into his new house mom helped him buy. But that same house mom then said was just perfect to rent for me and my family."* The mother masks her favoritism with constant statements on how fairly and equally she treats all her kids. Again, two maps.

Because the "right map" is perceived as the person, the map becomes the reason he or she does things. A caretaker is doing it to maintain the map, not to take care. A nice person is doing it to be seen as nice, not to render service. Navigators can get confused when they are trying to read these types of maps because all their effort is spent on validating the one map and hiding the other. The image of following the ideal map is promoted to cover up any exposure of the real usage of the hidden faulty map underneath. They want you to believe the outside map and not to see the other.

They betray who they really are by first confusing their personal map with themselves and being so ashamed of what they feel it says about them that they cover it up with another fantasized map presented to one and all as their real selves.

To help you, let all the validation be a tip off that things aren't as they are promoted to appear. Just read all the promotion and validation; it doesn't exist unless they have two maps with one covering up the usage of another. A person following an acceptable and workable single map doesn't validate or obscure.

The Big Cover-Up

Innately unattainable and based on an inherent lie, this "Right Map" never quite works, but the fear of having the flawed one underneath exposed is just too painful (to them it is exposing their flawed and erred self to outside scrutiny and judgement). The map's owner continually searches out and orchestrates situations and people to find evidence validating the absolute correctness and rightness of "The Right Map." They seem to be forever trying to elicit certain desired responses from these deliberately choreographed situations, even to the point of trying to cause specific emotional responses from specific people. This is what people do after adopting a "Right Map"; they orchestrate validation in support of it:

The inside map can't be changed or corrected with the outside map hiding its existance and usage. Unless these maps can be eventually separated from each other and from their owner, the navigator is stuck with just reading and reacting to their domination of another's life.

• Again from another colleague: *"Vicky is the corporate gadfly. Everyone talks to her. She is always into eveyrone's business and knows more about what's going on in the company that its president ever does. She always talks about building unity and an* esprit de corps *within the corporation. She is really just working on getting approval from others, but when something needs to get around the company unofficaly, we don't use a memo or announcement, we use her."*

The Fear of Losing Their Definition and Place in the World and Falling into Total Chaos

It seems that owners of this ideal right map are presenting a case to a judge, with key points for their side and supporting evidence for final judgement. This outer map seems to accelerate a self-damning process into a progressively downward spiral, getting more and more into making sure they are "right" and "enough." This validating frenzy cascades into a world of lies, with their becoming increasingly blind to seeing the truth about the separation between any of the maps and themselves. They are held in bondage to a world of their own making. The only thing that matters is protecting what is behind the outside map from view. If seen, they will have to accept a final judgement on themselves of how incomplete and errored they really are. Maybe worse, both the maps they have created will be invalidated, making their entire map-making machinery faulty. When this happens, they become totally lost, falling into complete chaos with no reference for who and what they are, where they are, and no hope of ever finding their way out.

Behind the facade of the right map is extreme fear, fear of losing their definition and place in existence, with no reference point to locate themselves or anybody and anything else, and fear of becoming totally lost with no hope of getting found. This can be extremely frightening, totally unacceptable, and lead to all sorts of protective and validating behavior over their "Right Map." Between both of these falsely perceived map extremes, the ideal map in front and the crappy map behind, is a measuring scale where the owners of both maps judge how they are doing in reaching the ideal along with others.

Many people have a facade from this **"Right Map"** of an adult, but underneath they still see the world the same way they saw it as a little child.

*Having a **"Right Map"** and also clearly reading issues related to it are impossible.*

An inescapable bind can occur when they can neither handle either map nor run from facing them.

To break this bind, outside intervention of some kind becomes inevitable.

• Ed is seen as a dynamo. His list of accomplishments goes on and on: he graduated with top honors at a prestigious university, he is a member of five corporate boards, advises the state innovation center, is a lay minister in his church, owns his own business, is a division head for a leading computer company, coaches little league, is part-owner of a race horse and is a gourmet cook. He just totaled his new car. It wasn't his fault, but during the accident the police checked on his license and it was revoked two years ago for too many speeding tickets. His foreign-born wife hates him to the point of showing the kids how to put catfood and hair in his dinner and not tell him (he hates cats and finding hair in his food). His kids are out of control, even though he has given them things he never had. The oldest son, with his wife, recently moved home after being fired from his job with his grandfather. Robin, the middle child, just got suspended for buying answers for his finals, and the youngest throws rocks at his partner's BMW. All this bothers his parents who think he isn't doing enough for his family. And he just lost his major accounts with the Navy, with all the cutbacks. Then to top it all off, last week he admitted himself to a rehabilitation center for drug abuse. He couldn't keep it up without chemical help, and even that turned on him.

99

The Validating Box

A Validating Box is created when the owner of a "Right Map" bends all surroundings into validation and protection for the map. When these idealized maps dominate a person's life, they coerce everything done, felt and thought into providing support for the map. This creates a very isolated box. separate from the larger reality. From the validating owner's viewpoint this becomes the entire world, but from a navigator's viewpoint it is only a box. A *Validating Box* is the severe reverse of the mapping process, where instead of a map being a representation of the actual world. the world becomes a representation of the map.

*Here is a **Validating Box** of Peter, a college professor:*

Dominates when it comes to teaching his subject matter. Says others should help him, but really won't let them.

Directs many meetings about his important field of work, including national chairman.

Has audiences with intellectual groupies that admire and worship him.

Involved in an on-going heated exchange with another professor, claiming he is not a qualified authority, doing very poor work verging on unprofessionalism.

I must be recognized as the top authority in my very important subject.

A topic in all conversations is about himself and what he is doing.

Implies often that men are much more able to do this work than women and becomes very agitated when anyone says differently.

Has a constant flow of important and noted people who contact him regularly, even at home.

Has a benefactor who funds him to do his extremely important work.

Manages to put his name on anything that would give him more notoriety.

Achieved tenure years ago and publishes regularly.

Managed public exposure on television in his field.

Peter's world is seen as the only world, and everything must mold to its demands.

A World in a Box of Their Own Creation

An idealized map (Right Map) once created will automatically make a very closed world of its own. **This map creates a closed world.** This world consists of validating support for the presentation of this "right map" as being the only true and correct map; covering up and hiding the other actual map from being discovered. To have this inside map brought into the light would open its owner to the shame of its errors and insufficiencies because this hidden map and its owner have been mistakenly combined. Into this world a navigator must often plot his course.

*While usually a map is a representation of the real terrain, with a "**Right Map**" the terrain is made into a represention of the map. This causes **Map Lockup**, not allowing any new map to be accepted and followed.*

"The nature of my friend's . . . incontrovertible evidence to her infant mind that she was "bad" is unknown to me. . . . (She) could not have tolerated any measure of good fortune for herself.

Within a few years she had had two illegitimate children, one by a man of another race, the other by an unknown man. She had taken several jobs that were, for her social background, humiliating; contracted poliomyelitis and thus became confined to a wheel chair for the rest of her life; caught tuberculosis while in the hospital for polio, ruining one lung and seriously damaging the other, dyed her hair an extremely unbecoming purplish red, which went far toward spoiling her persistent prettiness; and took up residence with a failed artist far older than herself.

When I last heard from her she told me with her usual gaiety that she had been clearing up after a party, had fallen out of her wheel-chair, and had broken one of her paralyzed legs.

She was never gloomy and never complained; she grew visibly more cheerful as disaster followed upon disaster. . . . I asked her once whether I was imagining it or if it was true that she was happier since becoming crippled. She answered immediately that she had never been happier in her life.

Half a dozen similar cases come to mind."[8]   Jean Liedloff

The validating box of another's "right map" may follow a different definition of what is "right" than ours, but this woman is now right within her world and is validated by it. Here are some signs to look for when a navigator comes across an owner of a *Validating Box:*

• **Validations of the "right map" are orchestrated.** They contrive events into providing evidence of their map's rightness. They are obsessed with causing only the responses they want from the "right map" and its superiority to the outside world so they spend incredible resources in attempting to control everything around them. Maintaining this image at all costs, they may get to the point of extorting evidence (forcing) to prove the right map's validity from situations and relationships. *"Its odd how Debi always manages these rush deadlines on key projects, one right after another. They involve people from all over the company. She becomes the center of it all; the corporate savior for a day. Yet, Sandy, with the same job, hasn't had one of these extravaganzas yet, and it has been years."*

• **Everything is included in validating their world with the "right map."** The "right map" is put onto the world around them as the

When validation becomes more important than truth, the maintenance of an image is chosen over having any real power.

101

Scapegoat: a biblical tradition where a goat, upon whose head the sins of the people are laid, is sent into the wilderness for punishment for their sins.

Scapegoating: blaming an innocent party for the shortcomings or failures of another; making someone responsible for something that he or she is not in control of.

only map there is. The universe is expected to conform to their map's description. Any inconsistency is dealt with by ignoring, controlling, using or attacking. Proof is taken no matter about the actuality of events. *"Everything I said to him while returning from the trip he took differently than I intended. I mentioned the failures, and he made them successes. I talked of things turning out differently with other choices and he said his choices were flawless. I even put him down, and he twisted it into praise. I finally just shut up and we drove the rest of the way in silence."*

• **Finding scapegoats to blame for any inadequacies found in the "right map."** Since the map is true and correct, but they are having problems implementing it, then someone or something must be at fault. This blame becomes a part of their "Right Map's" image management. *"If he hadn't mentioned to Ann that she had a choice to continue or leave, we would still be on the team together. We could have worked out our bad feelings. He is to blame for things changing." "It is her fault my feelings are hurt." "Allen is the reason my job was transferred to the Colorado office. I know, he retired two years ago, but if he had stayed, my sales would still be where they were."*

• **Judging where everything stands in relation to the "right map."** Because their map is believed to be innately superior and because they are the keepers of that map, they become the evaluators of how everybody is doing in relationship to it. Judgement is passed on everybody and everything, even themselves. *"This isn't my opinion, it is God's, and you're wrong!" "This isn't any way to run an office. It doesn't matter if they are the top in the region. There are set standards to be followed." "A report has no business looking like that. I know it was read and accepted, but that is not the correct way to do a report to the vice president. They should have checked with me to see if it was OK."*

Traveling in a Dangerous World Of Opportunity
These validating worlds are the most common kind of terrain the navigator will find so he should always be aware that when traveling into these worlds, things can get very treacherous. Once this ideal map has been adopted and so much invested in it (even viewed as themselves), maintaining it at all costs, then any loss of the map will be seen as a kind of death. Supporting their map and keeping alive the nonconflicting world around it becomes veiwed as life-preserving. The navigators must know about and delicately use the knowledge of their maps without exposing that knowledge. If they believe they are threatened, then the barricades will rapidly go up and cannons will fire, and you can't navigate easily in restricted waters. So travel a thin line between reading their world but not letting them know you know.

Validating Their Map to Travel Through Their World
This validating box is an entire world that is essentially a lie. Their whole exercise is a falsehood. They aren't their map. The "right map" is just a cover-up, and all the validation is just to keep the con going

The ability to discern clearly is in inverse proportion to the amount of validation. In other words, heavy validators are as blind as a bat with a bad head cold.

and avoid facing the fear of being lost. Expecting truthful interaction from the owner of a validating world is silly. The whole purpose of this box is validation; accepting that one fact will help you navigate through it more effectively. If the inside map ever really worked well, it probably did only as a kid, and certainly it doesn't work well now. But within that limitation there are opportunities. The way to deal with any validating box, with its "right map," is to read their map, and formulate a route through their validating world without threatening it.

Providing validation for another's maps can give you both credence and power within their world. But each situation is unique and your specific reactions must be customized to achieve the responses you desire. Here are what two people in differing situations did to get what they wanted through reading and validating maps:

A map is created to represent the world to find ones way through it, but when the map is loaded down with all sorts of personal fears and motivations, this map is then projected onto the world and the world is expected to conform to the map.

- Jim is a financial investor. He is getting a little paunchy and grey now, but still handsome. He is very articulate, well-mannered, and reads people's maps very well. Jim has made a good deal of money over the years doing basically only one thing. He reads his prospects world, sees what they want validated, then gives it to them in a neat package. Whatever they are validating, he presents ways to preserve it by investing with him. For example, if they seek self-importance through their kids, Jim shows them a way to make the kids even more important by investing with him. All the while he doesthis he is saying, "What incredible children. My kids could learn a lot by being around them, and so on." The money he is asking for is intertwined with their need for validation. These people receive two things fromJim. There are the financial returns they sometimes get and the verification of their world from a respected outsider.

  Some of these ventures have gone sour, but miraculously these people are so rewarded by his validation of their world that they don't hold him responsible for their loss. Many have even invested again and again in order to continue their relationship with Jim.

- Laura is one of the best business trainers I have ever seen. But the company she worked for never allowed her to fully do what she was capable of doing. She was always held back. It was subtle, but it was always there.

  In a presentation to the corporate heads, they were lavish in their praise of her abilities. Laura kept trying to break this invisible wall until one day she gave up and read the leadership's maps for what they were. It was a very chauvinistic company. Other male trainers even called themselves studs and if Laura was anything, she wasn't a stud, at just over five feet tall. The leadership wanted to take care of her, providing her with what she needed (taking care of the supposedly defenseless cute) up until it threatened their male egos. She was all right as long as she stayed in her place, but heaven forbid if she ever did better than they. In reading their validating box, she realized things where actually rigged against her success. Then deciding to use their condescending but helpful support and the facilities they provided, she navigated her way out of the company and into a job that gave her what she desired and the respect she deserved.

To a navigator a faulty map is just that. But to them it is them.

103

Entrapment

Entrapping is imposing one person's validating world (the "right map" and its surrounding validation) onto another. This is done by teaching selected outsiders the inside owner's "right map" and getting them to buy it as their "right map" too. Once the outsiders have bought the map, they then move in and take up residence in the box and begin jointly validating one another. One person tends to dominate this relationship, getting to set the rules on how this validating is done, but both are now caught in a closed world, often unable to find any way out again. They hold each other hostage to the support they need to avoid the exposure they now jointly fear.

An important validating interrelationship now exists, with both supporting the ideal while also providing the excuse for why the ideal has not arrived. This entrapping can keep going until it gets awfully crowded in there, capturing a group, an institution or even a nation into the box. These traps are all over the place, and a navigator should be careful in locating and steering quietly around them.

Entrapment takes three steps:
1. The trap is set when the bait is laid out. The bait is the ideal map.
2. When the victims buy into the bait (the ideal map), they are caught and reeled into the validating box.
3. Once inside, they bond together into validating one other in supporting the ideal and providing each other with the excuse why the ideal hasn't been reached. Both now work and set a trap to catch another, and the steps begin again.

These steps keep cycling over and over again until the end of the ideal map, acceptance of the actual map and separation of the map from the person or death, whichever comes first.

On a Soapbox

Entrapping another person into validating a personal map is an act of aggression. It is an assault on another human being. It is getting another to support an incorrect map because the maps owner doesn't have the courage to face the truth. Entrapment is a kind of possession and bondage. The rhetorical gymnastics used in supporting these validating worlds or boxes are very good and idealistic. always denying they're controlling, while all along they are. Always denying any other options as valid but theirs. Any navigators worth their wings or sails, or whatever they get, that get caught in one of these traps of baloney should be drummed out of the corps and made to walk the plank backwards with their head down. There, I've gotten that off my chest, and you have a view of my map. Now let's go on.

Entrapment is a hostile act of ensnaring another person into accepting the bait of an idealized map without any acknowledgement of the hidden map that is actually involved.

Entrapment is a lying game that always says it is telling the truth.

"What enables maps to advance a cause so effectively is the impression they manage to convey that they are precisely above such interest. They are convincing because the interest they serve is masked.

Despite an aura of neutrality maps present information selectively, shaping our perceptions of the world.

Every map is someone's way of getting you to look at the world his or her way."

Lucy Fellows
Smithsonian Museum Curator

An Opportunity and a Threat

To a navigator these boxed worlds are both an opportunity and a threat. The opportunity is that within these worlds their owners will do anything to have them validated. All the resources they have may already be going toward supporting their right map and its box anyway. So the navigator can use this need for validation to receive the things and actions he or she needs. But there is a negative side to these boxed in worlds: their traps are out and set. And as soon as you buy into any of these other maps, your effectiveness there is lost. So take great care in stepping around these traps. In these boxed worlds you are going to have to validate, or at least avoid invalidating them, while maintaining the integrity of your own map. What follows are some examples of entrapment:

• The following is a list of what is actually expected from a new husband I know after only a year of marriage. This is from a bride whose main map has to do with being a princess and being served. She was masterful in entrapping this guy and getting him to buy into her map. I wonder if the husband would have agreed to married her if he had known these rules beforehand:

 - I can criticize you, but in no way can you criticize me.

 - I get to do this criticism in public.

 - I get to use any of your belongings at any time without asking, but you have to ask to use mine, and do it nicely.

- I get to criticize and avoid your family, but you have to be with and can never criticize mine.

- We can discuss and evaluate important decisions, but I always decide when and have the final say.

- You are to take care of me and see that my needs are met, but whether or not I meet your needs is optional.

- The major goals of the family are mine to set.

- You have to tell me I'm beautiful, intelligent and nice, but I can tell you that there is much room for improvement and show you where.

- This is a story I just heard, and it's a lulu. I had met the person mentioned in this story years ago in a business situation, but things have certainly changed. *"Wayne is extremely intelligent. He is an inventor and a businessman. Has earned many millions of dollars over the years in his ventures. But a number of years ago Wayne had some religious experience which sent him into building an underground fortress in Nebraska. Something about the end of the world coming and he needed to be in a self-made, safe place with others he personally selects. Through a long sequence of events, I lived in his underground compound for three weeks (the storyteller has a history of going to the strangest places). On the surface things looked ideal, even angelic, and the followers flowed in working easily together. But after living there and working in the kitchen and not seeing the sun for weeks on end, I noticed how Wayne manipulated and controlled everything. I discovered he thought he was Jesus Christ (many people are doing that these days; pick a number and stand in line). Everyone was held in his subtle but ironlike grip. I even saw him strike his second in command for not following his commands exactly. His followers believed they owed their eternal salvation, and with his wealth in the business operated there, their financial salvation to Wayne. As long as they believed him, they were held by their own chains in this underground fortress, which was really just a prison. I also found out seven of the women in the compound were his wives. I quietly decided to leave and had no resistance, only a good deal of talk about what I thought God wanted. But when I started to talk to the others about what I was observing and what I felt was going on, I found myself hurriedly on the surface, with Wayne yelling orders about the drastic things that were about to happen. The huge metal doors at the entrance closed, and communication was severed. I found myself all alone on the surface with my few belongings."*

- My daughter's friend said this to her: "If you like me, you wouldn't go to Melissa's house, you would only come to mine."

- An overheard story that is too good of an example of entrapment to not include: *I had to go in for back surgery and needed a place to stay, and the only place I could go to recover was Mother's. I hadn't been getting along really well with her, but I had to go. The first few days after the surgery I was so out-of-it that I didn't notice anything, but later Mother was great and tended to my every need, slowly nursing me back to health. But as I got healthier and healthier, I noticed things about mom I had never seen. She keep saying, "You must stay in bed," "Don't do this or that, I'll do it for you," and "If you don't go very slow, you will end up back in the hospital." Her continual statements and actions keeping me in bed contradicted what my doctors wanted. One time, she actually pushed me back into the bed!*

The person who traps the other dominates the relationhip through his or her idealized "right map" which he or she has gotten the other person to accept.

YOU WILL APPRECIATE ME!

The key signal of entrapment is the attempt to control another's emotions and thoughts.

Beware telling others of a trap being set for them. They may not want to see it.

Just because you see the trap and can walk around it, doen't mean you have any responsibility to let others know of its existence.

The bait in the trap is the "ideal" or "right map."

I realized mother wanted me sick. She wanted to take care of me. A lifetime of service could be seen for what it was, self-service. She had even adopted an old retarded man who would never recover, to take care of him. She was like a vulture who fed on people's dependency on her, capturing and forcing them into her care. I got out of there as fast as I could to never return, except for occasional visits when I'm fully healthy to run out of the front door when I hear the words, "You don't look very well."

Beware of the Traps

Deliberately ensnaring another person in supporting a map that is known at some level to be flawed can, at the very least, deny growth and, at the very most, kill.

I went to my business one day to finish a project that had a final deadline in a few days. But when I arrived at work, one of the employees helping me on the project never showed up. For her not to call and let someone know she wouldn't be coming in was very unlike her. It was so out of character that another employee called her home and a few other places she might be, but to no avail. The next day we all found out what had happened. She had shot her husband. She had somehow gotten hold of his loaded a 45 caliber automatic pistol and emptied the magazine into him. He was a large, muscular man and even managed to live a few hours after. She had spent the time in jail, but was shortly released. She stated that he was extremely abusive of the kids and her and she didn't know what happened to get him shot. Coworkers, friends, family, public agency people and even the police seemed to be moved by her pleas of innocence. She stated she didn't know what happened and wasn't at fault. Over the following weeks she got money from the state, insurance, family and many others. She never returned to work; didn't seem to need to.

After all these years I'm still bothered by it. Oh, not about shooting; if he was as abusive as she said he was, it may have been her only way out. No, it is about her continual declarations of her unawareness to what actually went on the night of the shooting. Everything was so carefully and skillfully maneuvered to support her declaration of unawareness. It all seemed staged.

The intention of the human heart is difficult to ascertain, even in the best of circumstances. I wonder how many times the orchestrations of others trap us into believing a promoted ideal when what is behind it may be very far from the proclaimed truth?

Confirming one another's personal mindset maps within a relationship is both perfectly natural and desirable. Our mental health seems to depend on it. But there must be some allegiance between the people involved to something higher than just their maps for the factors of continued growth, improvement and adaptability to change to occur. These outside allegiances can be truth, the bottom line, survival, wisdom, real love, etc., just something outside everyone's map that can be used and agreed to as a criterion to evaluate the correctness of all the maps. Then with this outside guiding criterion, everyone's maps are more prone to be replaced or updated as dictated by changing circumstances.

The Collective Validating Box

For the last few pages I've talked about the biggest problems a *Change Navigator* will face in both reading another's map and determining how to route through his or her world. What follows is a summary of the sequence of ideas on this common map-reading problem leading up to and including this last unit. It features Walter:

1. Walter creates a map (personal mindset map) to understand his position and direction within the outside world.

2. Walter then forms a box containing his map, reflecting and confirming its description of the outside world. If this box is viewed as the outside world containing a map with no alternative, then—

3. Walter confuses his map with himself.

4. Since this map is flawed (all are), Walter also sees himself as flawed.

5. To cover his shame of being flawed, Walter then creates an ideal map (he also confuses this map with himself) to cover up his flawed map.

6. Walter then validates and promotes this ideal or right map as the only one he uses through selective supportive evidence he has gathered.

7. Walter then tries to entrap others into validating his ideal map by getting them to buy into his right map as their own.

8. Through entrapment Walter expands his box (**A Collective Validating Box**) to include on-going relationships for jointly providing evidence supporting their ideal maps and colluding between themselves in covering up the actual flawed maps everyone is using.

9. With this joint validation Walter may have created a collective and supportive box so rigid and unadaptive no change is possible from within, unless—

10. Outside circumstances can so totally invalidate the ideal maps and the hidden maps that they are seen as unworkable, and a viable outside alternative can also be seen; then change of the map is possible.*

Here is Walter's **Collective Validating World or Box** *with its colluding relationships of interlocking maps and supporting validations:*

- Ideal Map
- Interlocking Ideal Map Support
- Real Hidden Map

Walter's life is one of interconnected validating maps with his wife. Which creates an excusable facade to hide the real faulty maps being followed.

* Number 8 has to do with this unit, and number 9 and 10 have to do with the next section.

A Collective Validating Box may be a minimum of a couple of people and from there can include families, neighborhoods, towns, societies, cultures, companies and entire nations.

So locked into needing the verification of their rightness that they would be totally lost if they left their collective world.

Reading Behind the Group's Image

A *Collective Validating Box* is where individuals provide each other with evidence supporting their right maps, provide each other with the excuse why things aren't actually right, and provide a joint facade to hide of the actual maps being used. Entrapment sets up these kinds of relationships, and collusion keeps it going. People collude because they are jointly trying to camouflage and hide the truth from coming out—the truth that the maps are flawed.

They do this because of fear, fear of the exposure of being seen as flawed and the fear of losing the order their maps provide and getting lost in the chaos of existence. This collusion may provide the invisible adhesion in relationships that look on the surface like they should come apart, but continue on in absurd, ineffective and even damaging interchanges. It is the hidden glue that binds seemingly impossible situations together. The *Change Navigator* must read this underlying bond in order to know what is really going on within the relationships he has to deal with in traveling through this kind of world.

Reading the Hidden Cohesion Within Some Relationships

A common problem with being a *Change Navigator* is that in being an outsider you can clearly see, and may be repeatedly told by the persons involved, what the problem is and what needs to change. The solution is simple and easy, but when applied, it doesn't work and nothing changes. At the most, the navigator gets only a kind of pseudo change with a lot of activity, rhetoric and dust filling the air, but when it clears, nothing has really moved. Things are back to the way they were. What was missed and not read into the equation for change was underneath the surface—it is a factor called *Collusion.*

Collusion is a validating relationship (any two people, family, group, institution, nation, etc. . . .) where the individuals involved provide subliminal support for each other's heavily invested idealized map as the only map being utilized. Collusion masks the maps actually being used with maps that everyone is supposed to be following. Collusion is people helping each other in presenting facades of rightness for some outside approval. A martyr's map is, "I'm a righteous person for putting up with this persecution." The colluding persecutor's map is, "I'm right because they caused my problems, and they deserve to be punished." Each one needs the other to provide evidence to support the validity of his or her right map. The caretaker's map is, "I'm right to take care of this helpless person." The colluding invalid's map is, "I'm right, and because of the problems life dealt me, I deserve to be taken care of." Again, each needs the other for proof of rightness. Underneath all

THIS IS YOUR LUCKY DAY—WE ARE HAVING YOU FOR DINNER!

A Storm Warning:
The validating may become ruthless when those within the box attempt to control others' emotions and thoughts in order to validate their collective map.

The validating is ruthless when those within the box validated their own maps and are fulfilling their own needs under the disguise of some purported ideal.

this the people seethe with anger for having to do this to be enough and resent the other person colluding with them. In these relationships people are holding each other as willing hostages providing conclusive evidence of one another's most dearly held ideals. Collusion provides the cohesion in these relationships all within a validating world while protecting those colluding inside from anything contradictory—a self-locking prison for two or more.

A Joint Cover-up

With this strong evidence people in collusion can hide the fact that neither map matches much of the terrain anymore and that the map may be wrong and consequently they are. They can avoid having to face the pain of invalidation and being proved wrong on both the map and themselves. At some deep level those involved know that their maps are inaccurate, but the fear of losing their sense of place and definition in relation to everything they know and understand, especially themselves, is just too scary. Better to have a devil you know than the fear of facing the angel you don't know. Better the cover-up than the exposure.

• Ronald is the president of a very successful marketing company, and Richard is the vice president over advertising. Ronald never speaks kindly of Richard, with comments like: "At the very least he is incompetent. He does make a good example of what not to do. We need to find someone more capable to replace him; anyone who can tie their shoes with help from their mother would do." And Richard fights back with comments like, "Did he work for the Russian Army before he came here? Just spend another hour on the rack with the master torturer. If he is a leader, I'm the King of Norway." The places where these conflicting comments are made varies. With Ronald it is out in the open, even in meetings where Richard is present. With Richard it is always behind Ronald's back to others in the office. When these two are together, it is like they are jointly following some script. Ronald dominates and humiliates as he towers over the larger Richard, and Richard practices his art of groveling like some puppy caught chewing on his master's shoe.

For a long time I couldn't understand why these two had been at it for seven years. Why didn't they go their separate ways? It looked obvious that things didn't work for each of them. But it did work. Both needed the other as an excuse for their failings within this successful company. Ronald needed to dominate Richard and have an excuse for the problems around the company. Richard needed to be persecuted by Ronald to have an excuse for his failings. It actually worked quite well and is still going on.

• Long ago, when I still had all my hair, I worked for a family-owned business. Sanford was the company's president, and he hired his son to work in the business. His son was young, but pleasant and effective to work with. He even took our kidding on the benefits of nepotism.

A new corporate objective was centered on a program instituted within the company to increase sales in a selected area, and everyone was to support it. This son then came up with a good idea to do just that. It would have worked well. The son presented it to his father and the

The co-validating of "right maps" is used to cover the faulty maps actually being followed. Co-validating is manipulating each other into supporting the promoted image of a certain desired map as the only correct and right map being used.

other supervisors. Sanford accepted it on the surface, but when his son left the meeting after presenting his idea, the father said to everyone there, "Another lame idea, it will never work." To my surprise, Sanford set out to prove it wouldn't work. He commented negatively to a supplier, slowing down shipment of some needed materials for his son's idea. He withheld sufficient funds with a superficial reason why. Sanford even banded with the other supervisors deliberately diverting people to other projects, not support the new sales program. When it was all over, the son's idea died an agonizing death, and I even heard the words, "I told you so, son."

• This is from a friend after she returned from attending her grandfather's funeral. After the funeral everyone met at her grandparent's house where all crowded around her little grandmother, dressed in black, seated in an old chair. She kept moaning over and over again, "My dear, dear Lenny, what will I ever do without him? My sweetheart, you are gone."

Later that same day, my friend was alone with her grandmother when her grandmother's face suddenly changed. She raised her head and was staring at the wall where her husband's picture was hung. She showed uncharacteristic anger and suddenly cursed her deceased husband for all the affairs he had had over their years. This knowledge was unknown to my friend until that moment. Then a knock came at the door, and people again gathered around the grandmother as she continued to bemoan the loss of her "dear, dear Lenny."

• Stan, a colleague, complained about his family. They were all taking turns helping his mother ,who was sick. Or so she claimed. Stan said his mother, after the last kids, the twins, had been raised and left the house, had decided she had Parkinson's Disease. All the doctors denied this, but not his mother, who rapidly went from walking fine, to a walker, to a wheel chair and finally became bedridden. Stan was expected by all the family to care for his mother as she once had cared for him. This frustrated Stan to no end, and he said, "I love my mother but she doesn't have the disease. We are helping her die." Stan could do nothing to stop the momentum of care and collusion. He continued to help his mother through her disease on the days he was assigned.

A Box That Binds All Within to Supporting a Lie

Collusion within this collective validating box, because of the fear of acceptance of the truth about oneself, creates a steel web of counter-weighting validation linking all the people involved together. A narcissistic fantasy world created to cover the threat of exposure, blind to the reasons for its underlying pain. An act of lying to yourself and getting another liar to support it. A self-perpetuating system, incredibly pervasive in our society ,of wielding power but hiding unabashed weakness, indicative of some of the insane worlds the navigator must sail through.

And ye shall know the truth and the truth shall make you free.

John 8:32   111

Navigating

Charting and Following a Route Through Another's World

The more accurately a navigator can map the world of another, the more effectively he or she can traverse his or her territory. Most people never take the time to map the people and organizations they have to deal with. Even those who are critical in their lives. They just assume others see the world the way they do, or that they should see it the way they do. These people often stumble along blindly. This is fine in a house where nobody moves the furniture, but in our approaching future where drastic changes will be the norm, insight becomes mandatory. Some time devoted to reading another's maps can provide a navigator with enormous dividends, especially when compared with so little effort involved. While most grope around when interacting with others, a *Change Navigator* can do it with some degree of power. With the changes happening in our shared future, this skill of mindset map reading will become even more critical to both the navigator and those he or she is working with.

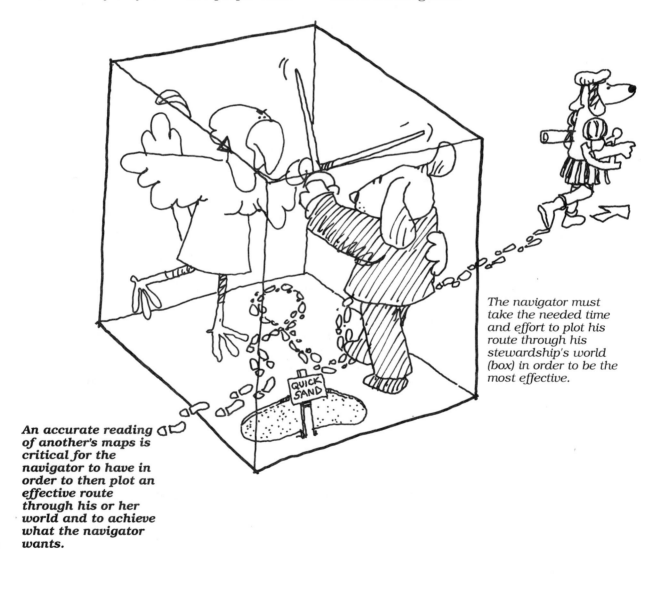

The navigator must take the needed time and effort to plot his route through his stewardship's world (box) in order to be the most effective.

An accurate reading of another's maps is critical for the navigator to have in order to then plot an effective route through his or her world and to achieve what the navigator wants.

QUICK SAND

When plotting a beacon on a map, two readings from different positions are taken. First, to determine the direction and second, where the direction lines cross to find location.

Accurate Map Reading may take different readings using different metaphors.

If a navigator can accurately read another's world (Box), he or she will be able to predict how this individual will react to certain changes that are happening or are going to happen in his or her individual worlds.

Mapping the Terrain of Another's Game

When mapping the location of a radio beacon, two readings need to be taken from two different locations. The first reading gives the direction; the second reading gives the distance. Also, when reading mindset maps of others, I've found taking the readings of another's map using two different analogies to be of great help. The first reading is taken using the analogy of a map and the like; the second reading is taken using the analogy of a game. Both together can provide a more accurate description of what is going on.

I have found using the analogy of a game to be extremely useful. It keeps open the needed objectivity to read things more accurately, and that is crucial when journeying through territory like I talked about. A navigator's effectiveness is determined by his or her accuracy. These individuals' and organizations' worlds are sometimes very difficult to navigate when you are too serious. Seeing things as a game being played may open things up to a clear view; so try the following change of viewpoint:

- Within the game world (the box) there is always a game being played.
- Warning: Don't get caught in their game. You can never win at another's game. You will always lose; they will bend their rules so it is guaranteed you will.
- To get out of the world of a game once you have caught yourself playing, you must accept losing whatever the game gave you.
- A person isn't his or her game or the world encasing it. The game is just the map he or she has bought and is following.
- Rules and behavior are always logical within the reality of the game world.
- Why the game came into being in the first place is unimportant. It is often wasted effort to even try to find out.
- What is stated is often opposite to the game being played. You can't depend on words used to promote a certain image.
- People naturally train others to play their game. Entrapment and collusion are all part of the game.
- The game always has a purpose.
- The game is affected by natural laws, whether they are considered, accepted, known or not.
- Talk to the players in the language of their game.
- The biggest need in a game is the confirmation and validation of its continued existence.
- Gamemaster: one who plays games for enlightenment, empowerment or control.
- If you want a relationship with someone, you must deal with his or her game and its world. Accept the baggage of the game if you want to interrelate with the player.
- Until the game doesn't work anymore there will be no change in the game. A game can only be replaced by another game (map).
- Emotional detachment is critical to reading and mapping the game. Your own game blinds you.
- The biggest trap is, "I don't play games, it's real!"
- Most games center on the central concept of not being enough or being right with themselves.

113

Questions to Better Read Another's Game

Ask yourself these questions when reading aothers' maps and when traveling through their world:

• What purpose does the game serve? What is it for?

• What do you do to win the game? What are the rewards to the players who play the game?

• What will happen if the game stops?

• What are the major players controlling in the game and for what purpose?

• What is the central metaphor of the game?

• What are the major relationships, and how do they work?

• What do you want from the game, and do you want to play the necessary game to get it?

• What are your interventions in changing the game?

Some Additional Ideas on Map Reading

• **Read between things, not the things themselves.** Read the relationships. Look at their relationship to the car, not the car. See how they interact with their partner; don't just see the partner. Look at how they relate with their job, not the job title and description. Take your readings through the patterns of interactions in the important relationships in their life: people, things, ideas, space, time, events, etc.

• **Read with the heart.** This process starts out with awkward readings of others' maps, but it ends with an unconscious holistic process that is naturally done without too much awareness. You can feel unsure of yourself when you've reached this point of naturalness. Don't ask yourself how you know what you know, because in our culture, if you can't explain something in words, it has no validity. Ignore it. This process is like learning to ride a bike, awkward and very much aware of everything at first, but then proceeding to the state where the bike becomes merely an extension of yourself like your legs. When this process reaches this state, you read with your heart, your feelings, and not your head. Recently, a person I was working closely with made an odd statement: "I will never turn on you." My feelings said he would, and I followed those feelings and separated myself from him, saving me some grief when they proved true.

• **Once you see, you can never go back again.** When you begin to read mindset maps, you may long for the innocence that you once had. What you are seeing can get a little raw. But you are just in the transition time, a kind of no-man's land where you don't belong anywhere, an in-between place that can be very frustrating. The world you are in may collapse from the discernment you've gained, but another world hasn't arrived yet to take its place. Press on; it will arrive and then the longing will stop. Coming is a world of power, and it replaces a world of powerlessness.

114

Map Reading Made a Little Easier

Because map reading may get very strange in very rapidly changing situations, I'm giving you some map reading examples using more conventional settings. I hope this will make the process of map reading easier to relate to and use in your life.

1. Situation: Grandma repeatedly states to the entire family, "I love you all the same." But between the siblings there is an ongoing battle over whose children are getting more attention from Grandma. This competition has even resulted in some very heated arguments and deeply hurt feelings in the family in the past. Reunions and family get-togethers are a hassle to see whose kids will be treated as fairly as Grandma says they should.

Reading: Upon reading Grandma's map with the pattern of what was really going on around her, one family found out something shocking. Grandma really didn't want much to do with any of her grandkids. She had recently been hired for a job she had wanted for years. She was really tired of grandchildren who were always messing up her immaculate house and tight schedule.

But Grandma had an image on her map that had to be upheld in her being viewed as equally loving to all her grandchildren, the ideal image of what a grandmother was supposed to do. So she kept saying how she wanted to be viewed by all the family as an equal-opportunity grandma.

Reaction: This same couple decided to get out of the fray. They read and accepted the reality of what was actually happening. They even showed their children the discrepancy between what Grandma says and what she does. This they did to try to lessen the continued pain in their kids about having all the competition equal. The kids reluctantly accepted what was going on at Grandma's house, especially after a few disastrous interactions.

This family keeps their distance from the fray, with only occasional visits. At first Grandma went crazy. She felt they didn't love her. But a sense of relief settled over their relationship with Grandma. It had been acknowledged that they loved her and that they wanted the best for her. They told her that they realized she had a tremendous burden and they only wanted to lighten her load by not demanding so much of her. Grandma realized that she didn't have to keep up the image any longer in this part of her life. The rest of the family seems to have gradually put this one family on the bench to watch the remainder of them continue playing the game: Who does Grandma like the best?

Comment: Considering the facts that the kids were being used as a way to keep score in the contest for attention from Grandma, and there was a good deal of turmoil between the various parents for equality, getting out of the entire game seemed the best solution. But since this competition was often a large part of what this extended family did, the couple that opted out ended up watching the game for Grandma from the sidelines.

2. Situation: John works in a department along with two other men of equal job description, age, seniority, etc. He recently found out through a reliable leak from the accounting department that their salary is almost twice his. John is very upset because he feels his work is comparable to theirs. John won't confront anyone with this discrepancy because, according to company policy, "He isn't suppose to know what other employees make." The hiring of both of the other men was influenced because they are sons of the company president's old golfing buddies. Also, the company is now changing the location of John's department to a another city.

Reading: John read his supervisor's map, and it states that his co-workers' value is greater than his because of their special relationship through their fathers to the company's president.

Reaction: John decides to move with the company anyway even when he accurately reads his supervisor's map about his worth to the company. But John's map states that he must prove his value. He decides that upon arrival in the new location he will throw himself into establishing his worth to his supervisor through long hours and hard work. He is going to prove himself irreplaceable. He feels he will have his goal, and his map will match the territory when he gets the raise he has been asking for.

Comment: I recently heard the head of John's department laughing and boasting with one of the two coworkers: "Whatever job we don't want to do we just don't do it and wait. Then John comes along and does it for us." The supervisor in John's department won't deviate from the momentum of using him in collusion with his co-workers. The three of them, the supervisor and the coworkers, have a game going among them to see who can get John to do what. John is starting to do some outlandish jobs now. Last time I heard, John did not yet have his raise and the other two who work with him are on a company trip with the supervisor. John is not on the trip with them; he is back at the office showing empty executive offices his abilities.

I'm always amazed at the ability of most people to cling to an old map until it becomes a heavily invested in fantasy, no matter how much evidence they have that the map doesn't relate to reality.

3. Situation: Michael, the head of a marketing department in a company I worked for, hired an outside motion picture production

A good rule of thumb with map reading: Always read first; react second. It is surprising how many of us react to situations by shooting first and asking questions later.

firm to do a film on a particular product. It was Michael's feeling that these producers had the ability to create a film so good that when it was presented to customers, they would immediately buy it. This intended film would be the key to increasing sales of this particular product, which had very sagging sales up until then.

Reading: Michael, the marketing vice president's, job is partly riding on his ability to save this particular product. His map dictates the need for a home run with a top selling product he is responsible for. He is basing his future success on what he considers is the considerable skill of these filmmakers. He admires their work partly because of his background, which was also in film. No product sales have been markedly increased by the use of film before, and it is highly unlikely this would increase sales either. Because of my previous unrelated work with these filmmakers, I read their maps. They demand whatever they are working on to fit their preconceived ideas. They are very hard to work with because they have all the answers even before the filmwork is begun. The filmmakers past efforts were always funded from foundation grants, not anything that has to produce results and make a profit. Though their work is good, it has always had this constraint. Also, hovering in the background is an executive vicepresident in another department who wanted marketing under his control. He has the map that he could do marketing better and wants an excuse to prove it. And he probably is right.

Reaction: I was in a dilemma: tell the marketing chief or keep quiet. After reviewing the situation, I decided to keep my mouth shut. I didn't say anything about what I thought about the filmmakers through past experience or the entire situation of the survival of marketing in its present form. Michael, the head of marketing, was a friend, but he had a history of scapegoating. And what was going on in his department had nothing to do with me. I felt I could get caught in all the changes that were going on.

Comments: The film people were let go. They wouldn't follow instructions. The film was never completed, and the one product's sales became so bad it was discontinued. Then, under increasing pressure, Michael resigned for another job. The entire department was obliterated and its functions given to the executive vicepresident who wanted to handle the marketing for the company. And I watched all this from a respectable distance.

4. Situation: Jed and Brent are two junior accountants who work for an accounting firm that is downsizing. They were both hired strait from a local university three years ago as the firm's workload was dramatically increasing. But now the company is beginning to shrink.

Reading: Jed believed management was going to reduce staff to save money by attrition and maybe a few layoffs, but not him because he was too competent. Jed never did check out the validity of this assumption. Brent, on the other hand, realized his job was at stake and became obsessed with finding out what was on the map of top management about the future of the company.

What Brent found on management's map was that they were going to take out the middle of the company by employing only the top employees with seniority and the bottom cheaper-salaried people. They felt this would make the company more manageable, competitive, and increase profits. The leadership had found that over 80% of their entire workload could be done by cheaper people working on computers, using a new sophisticated accounting software. This new computer software would dramatically reduce the need for a large professional staff. Any unique or specialized problem that cropped up could be handled by the senior accountant. In addition, accounts that didn't match this approach would be dropped. And this is the one idea that Jed could never buy into. He just couldn't believe that they would drop accounts. Brent read that management would need more help than they realized in setting up and managing the people on the computer. Brent saw an opportunity, but he must change his job from an accountant into a manager.

Reaction: For Jed it is business as usual. Brent trained himself on the new software in his off hours before anyone else inside the company. He then started a relationship with the key person that was to put this program into application and asked to be the first one. Brent was working himself out of a job. Through this he ended up training and managing people within the company. Jed ended up looking for a job.

Comment: Brent accepted what he had read on the company leadership's map and adopted it as his own. Jed read what he wanted to happen. The results proved which map was more viable.

Into a More Powerful Position

There is a power in accurately reading people's maps and accepting what is read. After reading their map, ask a very simple question: Given the map and the entire situation and all its constraints, what do I want? Consciously and deliberately finding out the parameters and constraints of the territory you find yourself in, and then carefully navigating a route through it, puts you into a more powerful position. My experience is that the majority of people don't know what the hell is going on and don't have the slightest idea how to find out. They don't even want to. They deny their own power in seeing things more clearly.

Remapping

Providing New Maps to More Accurately Navigate
a Changing Future

Late medieval times were hard ones for the Christian kingdoms of Europe. The Moslems had taken control of the Holy Land, and the Crusades were not dislodging them. It seemed that infidels were pressing on every side: Mongols pushing form the east, zealous followers of Islam controlling all of the Holy Land and North Africa, others holding a sizable foothold in Spain. These were bad times for the keepers of what was once the Holy Roman Empire.

The European kings, encompassed by enemies, longed for allies—other Christian kings who had succeeded against the Moslems in their own realms and who might be in a position to attack the infidels from the rear or on their flanks.

It wasn't long before the royal imagination got the better of the kings. After all, there really "should" be such a king elsewhere. Wasn't it a "fact" that St. Thomas carried the message to the fabled Indies? Surely something must have come of that.

A person or an institution will react differently to changing situations with a change in the map they are following.

Exactly how the rumors got started is lost in history. But by the twelfth century someone's imagination had created such a king: Presbyter, or Prester, John, a powerful and righteous priest-king who ruled a Christian kingdom somewhere in the unknown lands of the East. Grasping for every shred of evidence that Prester John was real, kings and pontiffs eagerly pointed to a "letter" from the distant king that appeared in western Europe around 1165—"proof" that Prester John not only existed but was eager to join forces with the Western kings to liberate the Holy Sepulcher. Medieval mapmakers started locating Prester John's kingdom, placing it somewhere on the unexplored fringes of their charts.

What is amazing is the durability of Prester John and his kingdom in the centuries that followed—even in the face of increasing evidence that the story was a myth. (No one seemed to ask how a mortal could have lived and ruled for centuries.) When Marco Polo and others opened contact with China and India, the whereabouts of Prester John was a subject of intense interest and inquiry. When confronted with strangers inquiring about someone who sounded like a threat to their rule, oriental potentates were quick to suggest that the newcomers look somewhere—anywhere—else, which further indicated that Prester John could eventually be found, but in some other place.

By the early 1400s, Europeans knew enough about the country eastward to finally realize that no Prester John had ever been there. But he had to be somewhere, didn't he? Maybe his kingdom was in Africa. The mapmakers moved the location of Prester John to the dark continent.

The dawning age of exploration was fueled in part by the desire to find him. Prince Henry the Navigator, of Portugal, had his sea captains looking for contact with the elusive king as they moved down the west coast of Africa, before eventually sailing on to India. Even as late as 1573, the best Dutch maps of the world showed Prester John's kingdom in what is now Ethiopia. The long-lived priest-king who "should have been" died hard.[2]

The Typical Process of Gradually Changing Maps

The maps of Prester John are an example of the usual map-changing process (with a real map). It is a very slow process of receiving conflicting evidence and responding with modifications to the map. This gradual updating of the map keeps going until the negating evidence becomes so insurmountable that finally the complete map must be discarded for a new more accurate one. Like with the Prester John map, these central kinds of motivating maps often begin as a counterweight to some major fear and hoped for solution. They are replaced only after conflicting territorial facts stack up so high that they are finally crushed to death.

This is the slow way the remapping process usually takes place, but with the dramatic changes happening in our society, we can no longer afford its luxury of time, patience and stubborn resistance. Continued use of outdated maps may damage fragile situations as they travel at incredible speeds. It is one thing to follow an incorrect map when you are only going a few miles a day over ocean or land; it is quite another thing to use it when you are going thousands of miles a day in the air. Intervention and an intervening agent are

It is one thing to have an erroneous map when you are riding on a camel; it is quite another thing to have one when you are riding in a spacecraft.

120

*The **Change Navigator** can function at the level of simply reading the maps of others and routing around and through them, or he or she can function at the more active level of changing their maps.*

The imminence of ignoring an incredible opportunity or of facing total disaster may help him or her make that choice of what level the navigator functions at.

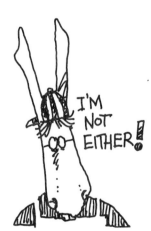

A few points before beginning:

• There is only one content map used in this entire section to present the remapping process.

• The remapping process has only one objective: to provide an alternative map better than the one being used and one more adaptable to change.

• It is always their choice if they accept a new map or not.

called for in such times, moving people into actively replacing and searching for viable alternatives to their present maps. Our survival and continued ability to even respond to change is at stake.

Intervening To Change Mindset Maps

The *Change Navigator* can function at the level of simply reading the maps of others, then using that knowledge to route a course around and through the map owner's world, or the navigator can function at the more active level of changing their maps. This is to do more than understand another's viewpoint; it is to help them consider that which they have never considered, that is, to totally change their viewpoint by adopting a different map.

When working on a farm years ago, I learned that when you find a tree stump in the field, you have two options: you can plow around it or spend the effort to remove the stump and plow straight. In the previous section we just went around, but in this section we go straight. The purpose of the last section was to read the map and then plan effective routes accordingly. In this section the purpose is to read the map and then intervene and change it.

Some examples of individuals who where *Change Navigators* involved in the map-changing business (Remapping):

• Thomas Jefferson who, with a price on his head, forged new ideas into a document that changed the world.

• Rachel Carson, a biologist, who first brought to the public awareness the damage mankind was doing to the natural environment, particularly with pesticides. In a calm manner she presented evidence that became overwhelming, and society's map and responsibility began to move.

• Buckminster Fuller, the engineer and designer who invented the geodesic dome. From a brush with suicide on a Chicago bridge, he decided to commit "egocide," as he defined it, and proceeded for the next 50 years to tirelessly change our maps. "Spaceship Earth" and "synergy" are Bucky's terms.

• Ralph Nader, a consumer advocate. Much of our concern over product safety in our automobiles and consumer products we owe to him.

• And one last navigator is Larry, a business partner, who once asked me the question, "How do you do what you do? When you do things a certain way, you are great, never seen anyone better. But when you don't do it that way, you're a real jackass." Good question; it changed the direction of my life.

We often curse these navigators and consider them to be a nuisance and troublemakers as they lead us down a new path. But when it's all over, we honor and thank them. Navigators give us options and alternatives to our present direction, showing us a way out of where we are into something more. You're a full-fledged *Change Navigator*, like the ones mentioned, if you want to help someone into somewhere more than where they now are. Here is how.

121

The Remapping Process

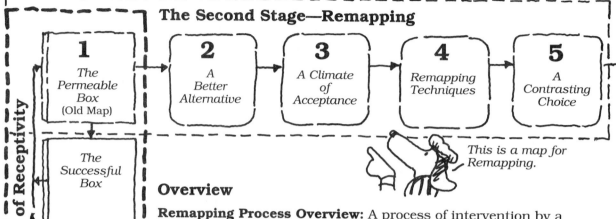

The Second Stage—Remapping

1	2	3	4	5
The Permeable Box (Old Map)	A Better Alternative	A Climate of Acceptance	Remapping Techniques	A Contrasting Choice

First Stage—Levels of Receptivity

The Successful Box

The Superior Box

The Fear-Filled Box

The Hostile Box

The Collapsed Box (Unresolveable Bind)

This is a map for Remapping.

Overview

Remapping Process Overview: A process of intervention by a *Change Navigator* into another person's world to cause perceptual change. The navigator does this through a deliberate exchanging of the person's present mindset map with a new map which is more accurate in representing the outside world. This intervention is for the purpose of changing the person's responsiveness so he or she can better adapt to increasingly rapid change.

Remapping is a two-stage process: The first stage contains the level of receptivity to accepting the possibility of another map to guide their choices. The second stage is the sequence of steps involved in moving a receptive person from the old map to the new one.

Stage One—Levels of Receptivity

This level of acceptance is indicated by this vertical series of boxes. These boxes represent the degree a person is willing to be open to map changing. Descending from there are the progressively hardening walls of boxes, the barricade against outside contradictions. Dropping vertically from an openness on top are the worsening stages of closing minds into closed worlds (map boxes). These boxes vary from an open permeable box on the top, through various closed boxes, into one at the bottom that represents the failure of their encased map to accurately describe the outer reality.

This sequence begins with a permeable box containing a malleable map. But once the owner has success with this map, things can quickly change. A successful map is often wanted to be viewed as reality, not just accepted for what it is—a map. The map may be seen as an example of how superior or right its owner is. But when outside contradictions appear and threaten this superiority, the fear of losing it arises. They may have invested so much of themselves in their success that when failures or flaws appear, they fear not having this map and thus the reality. With this fear the first reaction

122

* There is a third stage, but it is too unconventional in its approach even for this book.

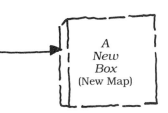

*A
New
Box*
(New Map)

This is the stage where the new map is adopted and consequently a new box is created. When things change and this new map becomes inaccurate, the whole remapping process begins again. Map changing is a continual process.

is to protect and maintain, but when that doesn't stop the escalating threat, they may then attack what is threatening. Each of these responses is a separate box leading to the last box. This is the final box that collapses from the complete failure of the map to reflect what is actually going on. Then when the growing inadequacies of the map can no longer be ignored and the outer world invalidates their map with ever increasing effectiveness, their map's world or box collapses of its own pressure from this encroaching outside reality. This collapsing causes a point of choice—the death of something or findinf an outside alternative. And the question indicating this desired change that may arise is, "Is there another way?" This question happens when the order provided by the map is in conflict with the maps, increasing failure to represent reality and the map becomes too painful to continue using. Then a way out may be wanted; intervention is desired, and the box is permeable again.

Stage Two—Steps For Remapping

The numbered steps going across the page represent the steps involved by the Change Navigators in helping another change their mindset maps, thus creating a different world for them with different responses.

1. The Permeable Box (The Old Map) The only box or world in which a navigator can begin the remapping process is with a permeable box. The remapping begins with an openness in considering a replacement or modification on their existing map with an outside alternative presented by the navigator.

2. A Better Alternative The outside map favored by the navigator must be better than the old one being used. This new map must be a more accurate representation and description of the changing world. It must be a viable alternative. It is the responsibility of the navigator to make sure it is, even before presenting it. A better map initiates the need to change a map, but it is crucial to the entire remapping process that it is better.

3. A Climate of Acceptance The navigator should try to help create an open environment for the other people so they will be willing to consider outside alternatives from the navigator. This is best done if they are made aware of a proven history of new maps from the navigator which produce desired results.

4. Remapping Techniques There are specific methods for the navigator to use in providing the link between the old map and the new. There are ways to help them understand things they may not have ever considered—a map beyond their present concepts, techniques to connect the person's problems to a new map's solutions.

5. A Contrasting Choice Show a clear contrast for choice. Present the new alternative map in juxtaposition with the old map. Present the old problems with new solutions. Show them the map and the way out into new territory.

New Box, New Map

Now, the entire process begins again with a choice of accepting the map as changeable or investing in its rightness and continuance.

REPLACING AN OLD MAP WITH A NEW ONE

First Stage
Levels of Receptivity

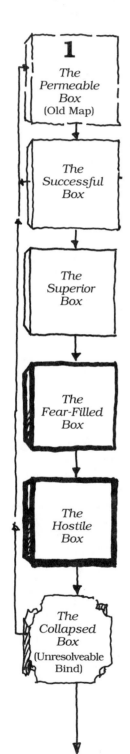

1

The Permeable Box
(Old Map)

The Successful Box

The Superior Box

The Fear-Filled Box

The Hostile Box

The Collapsed Box
(Unresolveable Bind)

This part of the **Remapping Process** is about the box (a map and the world surrounding the map) as progressive stages of reactions to the probability of changing the map inside. The only stage that can be remapped is the one open to adaptation on the top end. The other descending box stages are the increasing protective measures to maintain the map inside. Finally, at the bottom box the map's inadequacies become so overwhelming that to continue supporting it becomes too damaging. The bottom box must move back into the open box on top and accept changing the map or face the death of something linked to it. These boxes are the degrees of receptivity to map changing that the *Change Navigator* must learn to read, then navigate into the most receptive stage for the remapping process to begin. **The navigator can only do the remapping process with the top open box or when a box has collapsed and is brought back to that beginning stage.**

One thing to remember as a navigator is that these levels can intermix depending on the situation. A person may have a permeable map in one area of his or her life and a collapsing map in another. Also, a person may have a successful box at one time and a permeable box at another. These box levels can be in a state of flux depending on changing situations and settings, but the general pattern does seem to be consistent. Here are these boxes in greater detail:

The Permeable Box: Maps are not the territory. The road you drive over in your car is one thing and real, but the map in the glove compartment is another and it isn't. It is only a schematic of the road, not the real road. A map is only an approximate representation of the terrain; it can never be anything more. The mountain on the map can never be the real mountain. Humans seems to have a natural weakness concerning this one point. They are constantly mistaking the map for the territory and making the box that contains and reflects the beliefs of the map into becoming the real world. Since maps are only approximations, they will always be changing and modifying. Rand McNally seems to understand this with the constant updating of their maps, but the rest of us often forget that we must do the same.

The only map and its encompassing world (or box) that accepts this truth about maps is the permeable box. This box is open to a continual process of enlarging, modifying, accepting of new maps.

__The Permeable Box__ is one with unhardened and open walls created from a map that is accepted as needing updating and maybe replacement. This is the only box that mirrors the fact of what a map really is.

All the other kinds of boxes are progressive responses to the increasing fear of being wrong, flawed and lost.

The Successful Box
Success in having the map totally confirmed can lead to the belief that it isn't a map.

Alternatives are nonthreatening, and things aren't absolute. This is the most stable and truthful box, especially during times of accelerating change. This box may be in one part of an individual's life and not in another part, and it is the first step in the remapping process. A list of factors to maintain a box's permeability:

• Must hold to something higher than and outside their box.

• Recognize maps are always approximations.

• Give up validating and protecting self-importance through a set map.

• Deal with and accept the fear of the unknown.

• Accept change as a constant and that any other map not accepting this fact is automatically building on a falsehood.

• Won't confuse a faulty map with themselves. Accept the reality of what and who they are.

• Must be open to consider the probability of eventually accepting maps that they are not even aware of.

The Successful Box: A personal governing map totally confirmed by its surroundings. This box offers no or few contradictions; everything is working well and everything says the map inside is correct. The forward momentum of success (even if only in the past) is the hardest map to change because there is no reason to change. If something works and works well you don't tend to get it fixed. As with the law of physics, once a body is in motion, it tends to remain in motion and headed in the same direction. The reason why many once-successful people and organizations eventually fail in changing times or in entering new ventures is that they can't see any alternative to their once-successful map. Success keeps you from noticing alternatives, but you will eventually have to face change as everything changes.

The most dangerous human experience can be success because the map that caused it may be adopted by its owner as himself or herself, then made into an ideal image to hide deep feelings of inadequacy linked into another hidden map that is actually being followed. When this successful map becomes the ultimate proof with a camouflaging superiority, it turns into the next kind of box. About the only thing a navigator can do with this box is to read the map and wait until something happens or can be made to happen to cause contradiction in this box's confirming evidence. To illustrate:

• China is the oldest relatively successful culture in history. It has existed in some form for thousands of years. China is still around, while the Roman or Inca empires aren't. Three inventions that changed the world were all invented by the Chinese: gunpowder, the compass and movable type. In China gunpowder was used only in ceremonies, movable type was not viable with the language using too many characters (over 1,000), and since travel was restricted by authority to coastal areas, the compass wasn't needed. Western

Europeans adopted all these inventions and expanded their use and application in warfare, exploration and mass printing, thus changing the world—even China.

- Elizabeth is the most abused person that I know that is still alive to tell about it, and she almost wasn't. But she has never left her fantasy world. I believe it kept her alive and sane when she was a child in an environment that was severely warped and dangerous, but that place no longer exits. She can't let go of what worked and worked well in the past. The momentum of a successful childhood map continues to this day. But now it is hurting her by thwarting her power in an adult world.

- The Swiss watch industry used to dominate the world market for timepieces. In the early 1960s a consortium of the Swiss watch industry, in their research department, developed electronic quartz timing. Up until then all watch's timing was mechanical. The consortium could see no need for this new timing when the mechanical timing did so well in their very successful industry. But the invention was taken to a trade show and seen by two companies, Texas Instruments and Seiko. Within a few years the Swiss lost their industry dominance to the electronic watches of the Japanese.

The Next Boxes

Early mapmakers, when they finished drawing in all the territory that was known, filled in the remaining part of the map from their imagination. Beautifully illustrated out in the uncharted seas were fantastic creatures waiting to devour any ship that happened upon them. There where usually the same words that marked the line between charted lands and the unknown. And they were, "Beyond this point there be dragons and monsters."

When contradictions arrive from beyond an individual's known world, imaginations also run wild as with the early mapmakers. Facing the same fear of the unknown, people conjured up images of the unknown with monsters and dragons of their own making. Maps create order and meaning, and we all have a deep need for those things to make the unknown known. Without our maps we are lost and in chaos, and not knowing where or even who we are is a scary proposition. All the following boxes are degrees of protecting the map contained inside against its invalidation and avoiding the fear of facing the unknown.

If navigators can read an individual's map, they may be able to predict what kind of protective box will be created by the individual in reacting to approaching changes. With this knowledge navigators can thus adapt themselves to more effective responses when interacting with this person, perhaps even instigating events that will bring this individual back to a more open and accepting state.

The thicker the walls of a person's box, the greater the inability to see the obvious.

The Superior Box: A box with a map that is considered totally right or better than anything else. Once a map is successful, it is easy to invest oneself in it and believe in being innately superior to mask

The Superior Box
The more absolute the map, the more superiority will be exhibited.

inadequacies underneath. This box is created when the successful box is seen as the way things really are. The box becomes the only reality and is seen as indistinguishable from it.

This box can get even worse when the map is considered absolute, perfect, and the only "right" one. After all, how could anyone offer an alternative to superior perfection, a place where there are no alternatives because there isn't anything else. Anything that is different or contradicts this map must be evil or crazy. This box and their understanding of it completely becomes the world and the way things work. Since they understand this world, they can now pass judgement on themselves and everything else. They are in control and dominant.

You as a navigator can't directly teach people who are superior. There isn't a map you have that can outdo theirs. So, you can only wait until their superiority is brought into question. Even someone on a luxury liner having a lobster dinner with the ship's captain, while dressed in formal attire, can be made to take a trip in a row boat—if the ship starts to sink. The following story will illustrate what I'm talking about with a superior box and how far it can go:

- I've had some limited exposure to computer programs and hardware called virtual reality. They are interactive computer programs that put you *into* the world of the computer. The world of the computer is made almost real. With games now you more or less stand on the outside and manipulate something inside the game. With these programs you go into the games by putting on a hat with small screens and stereo sound or enter a simulator. Then you fly a vehicle that never leaves the ground, but from your windows you see the trees and houses below, and as you respond, the vehicle responds with the images and sounds changing to match. You become an intelligent monster bug on another planet, interacting with other bugs and walking that world, destroying as many of the enemy bugs as you can along the way.

One of the worries of these kinds of ever increasingly realistic games is that people will get lost in them. They would rather be in the computer's world than in their own. I can see why; they couldn't pull me away from the ones I used. I got completely taken up in the new world. I could be a superior warrior in there, but just a frump out here.

Why this worry about these computer programs is so very real to me is that I watched something happen. Aaron is a kid with a genius I.Q. and he is completely into games and computer games. He would spend all his free time doing them. The only time you could engage him in an intelligent conversation was when this was the subject. Aaron's whole life gradually evolved around these games until I believe his mother lost him. When outside situations at school and home increasingly failed, he dropped more and more into his game world where he could succeed. In there he could play God. In fact, he could be God.

Within the program he was a success. Within that world he was superior. The personality within the games seeped out into his life. The line between reality and the game became lost. Everything and everybody became part of the game worlds he constantly created and interacted in. His failures in life dramatically increased. At this point, I

127

lost contact with Aaron. I don't know what became of him. I don't know if he came back.

The closed worlds of a person's mindset map are like these simulated worlds of the computer games. The map's world becomes real like the electronic game's world becomes real. They have similar addictions and consequences when seen as totally real, with the players becoming masters in a world of their own creation. Then begins a downward slide into a harsh confrontation with reality.

The Fear-Filled Box
Real power is based on what is actually happening over any map. We resign ourselves to powerlessness when we choose an old map over a different territory.

The superior box can be changed if there is sufficient power over the entire context to impose a change on it to the point of invalidation of their map. If you own some key element or control the supporting confirmation in their life, you may be able to force a change. A parent or a manager can enforce his or her control over the world of his or her charge to make things change. But when things are riding high for someone and you are seen as the one who cut things down, hatred and a war of open or subtle confrontation are often the results. Intervening to cause perceived failure of an ideal demands an excuse, and someone forcing things can provide that excuse.

In many situations all the navigator has to do is wait. Things are changing so fast that a superior map naturally isn't that way for long. The next boxes may be only a sneeze away.

The Fear-Filled Box: When it is known at some level that this mask of superior "rightness" is faulty, the deeply hidden inadequacies surface. The loss of the ideal map uncovers the erred map underneath, and because both maps have been confused with themselves, this is taken personally—they are faulty. The fear is of being exposed and losing any maps that follow. Their means of achieving order and meaning in their lives is being proved invalid—they face becoming totally lost. To avoid this, the box becomes a fortress with thick, rigid and unyielding walls for protection against the pain of exposure. They become increasingly withdrawn, often running headlong into a fantasy world of pretended validations and imagined scapegoats. They pace back and forth within the box, searching for the total confirmation that must be there, but isn't. If the threat continues, they proceed into the next type of box. Some examples of the fear box are:

• After the divorce, when everything she had invested in was seen as wrong and crumbling, she frantically scanned every part of her life to find a solution. She found it in her early adolescence, when she was 13. It was the high point of her life. She rebuilt everything as it was then, even to the point of moving to the same place she had lived at 13, into the same house and doing the same activities. She acquired the viewpoint of a teenager. You could only interact with her on that level. Increasing even this reaction caused problems, and she acquired a siege mentality, fortifying herself against all contradictions by severing herself from close contact with anyone emotionally older.

- He had invested years of intense study and research. But when his previously accepted theories were questioned by leading experts, things happened. He went on a binge of frantic evidence gatherings to support his now-questioned map. Anything and everything was bent, construed and forced into something that would tell him he was right. If you said or did any little thing around him, it became proof he was right. No matter what it was.

  When something went against his opinion and couldn't be crushed with this proof, he seemed to isolated it with little airtight compartments within his mind and ignore it. He was so brilliant his intellect could set up circumstances that would ensure anyone opposing's failure. With his articulate manner and extensive comprehension, others would be deliberately set up to lose any argument. He did this so he could say to himself with a sly smile of his pretended superiority, "I gotcha!"

- A business colleague of mine, years before I met her, had one of those affairs-to-remember. One day she started reminiscing and recalled the last statement she had heard from her former lover: "I've never been so alive as I was with you, never so much of my real self. The marriage is a sham. Even my wife admits that. But the fear of the family business and the kids and others, reaction and . . . I will pretend everything is all right and I'm happy. I know I can; I've been doing all it my life."

The Hostile Box: The box becomes less like a fortress and more like a tank. Fear transforms into anger. Everything is considered either a support to their map and their world or dangerous to it. They attempt to eliminate any threat of conflicting evidence to keep the map safe. They become hostile by frantically extorting evidence to shore up the status quo by actively entrapping others into providing proof of the rightness of their map. They banish from their world anything that continues to contradict them, blaming it for the conflicts they are having. They can't afford to be wrong. The more absolute and perfect the map, the more driven in these actions they become, even to the point of aggression by forcing others to follow this invalid map through threats. But if the faults in the maps become overwhelming they turn into the next box. Here are some examples of this box:

The Hostile Box
The people inside the box, if threatened enough, will separate anyone advocating an alternative—divorce, firing, separation, excommunication, suicide or murder. So beware, navigator!

- I used to live near Brian, and one day he related this story. Brian worked for a very large foundation as a junior accountant. This foundation was quite successful, and donations were at an all-time high when he was hired. He was new at the job and made some assumptions that when he made reports he did his best at doing them accurately and honestly. But when he gave an internal report, he was pulled aside by his boss and threatened with firing. It seemed that within the foundation the internal reports were doctored to look a certain way. He expected to see the outside reports done that way; they are often just window dressing anyway. But not internal reports. He questioned his boss, "How on earth can you make clear decisions in an organization when you don't have accurate and honest data?"

  Brian never received an answer and soon learned not to questioned the established procedure. Fear had seeped through the entire accounting department. If you didn't bend the figures to make the vice presidents feel good, you were soon gone. This was a successful

"There is no safety in numbers or anything else."

James Thurber

organization, and the accounting department was to provide the figures to prove it.

But when donations began to decline, things got even worse. The entire department's climate became one of fear, extreme pressure on anyone with integrity to consistently present the hoped-for ideal at the expense of communicating the truth. Brian was forced to quit and left for another business more sane.

• In 1848 Ingnaz Semmelweis, while working at a clinic, developed the simple technique of having a physician wash his hands in a chlorine solution prior to delivering of a baby. It immediately reduced the maternal mortality rate in the clinic from 18 percent to only 1 percent. This simple procedure reduced the death rate of new babies at the clinic by over 90%.

But twelve years later, in 1860, in the same clinic, over 1/3 of the mothers died giving birth, and Ignaz Semmelweis, the father of modern surgical sterilization techniques, ended up committing suicide in a mental institution. What had caused this drastic change in events? The doctors and their supporters branded him a fake, a disrupter, someone who had extreme political views, and then returned to the same medical procedures used in the past.

• A threatened set map is why Christ and Socrates were branded evil and were killed.

• *"The biggest fear within our present educational system is being surprised and outclassed by another superior system. That is why they will always thwart any outside alternative,"* asserts a state school board member.

• Fear induces a tyranny of the ideal map. When people or institutions think that their way of seeing things is the only way and it is threatened by an alternative map, then they set out to enforce their viewpoint and stamp out any credible opposition.

"What happens when one has striven long and hard to develop a working view of the world, a seemingly useful, workable map, then is confronted with new information suggesting that the view is wrong and the map needs to be largely redrawn? The painful effort required seems frightening, almost overwhelming. What we do more often than not, and usually unconsciously, is to ignore the new information. Often this act of ignoring is much more than passive. We may denounce the new information as false, dangerous, heretical, the work of the devil. We may actually crusade against it, and even attempt to manipulate the world so as to make it conform to our view of reality. Rather than try to change the map, an individual may try to destroy the new reality. Sadly, such a person may expend much more energy ultimately in defending an outmoded view of the world than would have been required to revise and correct it in the first place."

M. Scott Peck
A Road Less Traveled

Don't confuse a change in address for a change in maps. *Just because it is a different job, a new marriage, another situation or a move in location doesn't mean their map has changed in the least.*

The Last Box

I've found that once people invest their personality in the perpetuation of a map, even against credible contrary information, they usually won't change it until they digress into this last box. The only way their map is possibly replaced is when their map fails. When a person's world slides into this last stage, it is time for the skillful intervention of the *Change Navigator*. They can help turn a person around into a more receptive state where the remapping process can begin. This is where change works to the advantage of the navigators and what they are trying to accomplish in changing another's maps. Their most important ability here is timing.

The Collapsed Box
All the maps don't work, and reality crushes the box.

The Collapsed Box: The outside reality crashes down onto the inside delusion. The consequences of using obsolete maps have arrived, and the map's invalidity becomes increasingly undeniable and overwhelming. The maps no longer accurately represent the territory the person is now in. The maps simply don't work anymore. They are bankrupt, wrong and unworkable. Where there is supposed to be a mountain according to the map, they are in the middle of a lake. Where there is supposed to be a certain result they have the opposite.

Not only are the maps false, but the box's owners' entire map-making machinery is being proved invalid. They now feel totally lost without a map or any way to make one and fall increasingly into chaos. They seem locked in a collapsing prison of their own making. Examples of this collapse:

People drowning in their own validation, madly treading water, hoping to stay afloat, can stay there for a very long time. But in a storm treading water is infinitely harder.

• With the takeover and the arrival of new management, Malcolm faced a different future than he had anticipated for all those years of working for the same company. He now lived in a world he couldn't predict or understand his role. He acted like an expressionless zombie following established instructions and procedures to the letter.

• Russian communism collapses. The Bolshevik Revolution of 1917 runs out of steam, the empire disassembles and alternatives are sought. A family member just returning from six months in Russia spoke of what the people she lived with wanted: *"The government to them is distant and inept. Their worry is how to make it through today."*

• What if this happened? *The nutty neighbor had been talking about the purple aliens arriving from space and removing everyone in the area for their scientific experiments. He had continued to bring it up ever since he moved into the house seven years ago. He livened up the mundane activities of the day with his wild but harmless stories. Then as she stared out the kitchen window after cleaning up from supper, the huge craft suddenly appeared and hovered above the nutty neighbor's house. Then out came the nutty neighbor with a loud speaker calling all the neighbors to prepare to depart.*

• IBM posted a 1992 loss of nearly $5 billion, up to then the largest drop in earnings for any corporation in U.S. corporate history. Time for a map change?

The Bind That Demands a Change
The important factor causing change in a collapsed box is the pain of an *Unresolveable Bind*. This is where within the constraints of a person's world or box there is no solution to the problems faced. There should be, but when any solutions are tried, things seem to just get worse, not better. A situation seems impossible to work out successfully by utilizing any existing maps known

The Collapsed Box
When the pain of the bind in the box becomes too much to accept and a possible alternative outside the box is desired, things revert to the beginning box and the start of the remapping process.

by the person in the box, but it is seen as all they have to guide them. The instructions on the map demand to be followed, but it only leads down a logical road back to where things started, an eroding cycle in an increasingly painful and frustrating dilemma. Examples:

- Unrestrained growth produces the optimal economic growth for a better life, but pollution from the growth destroys the quality of the better life.

- "I'll only allow you to work here if I can trust you, but you have the qualifications I'm after. But how do I know you are not deliberately being honest to get the job permanently and then you will steal from me? I don't know if I can trust you."

- Tracy wanted to be mistreated so she could be justified in her map describing her husband as insensitive, but at the same time she wanted him to be more sensitive.

- You are caught in the desert without any water. The map shows water up ahead to the north. You travel north but end up even farther into the desert without anything to drink. You look at the map again and it shows water to the north.

- Her map dictates she is a princess and should be treated as such. But she has the need for companionship that can only be met by another. She goes to a person for companionship, expecting to be treated like a princess. Instead he reacts to her superiority and become is even more distant. Her need for friendship becomes even more acute.

The Unresolvable Bind Worsens

The airtight world continues to collapse from the increasingly inaccurate maps being followed. It is time for a choice: hold on by your finger tips for just a little while longer hoping for a prescribed miracle, resigning to the hopelessness of it all, or question the possibility of an unknown outside alternative. In the end with complete map failure, finding an alternative to their invalid map or facing some form of death is their only choice. Death in a relationship, death in an industry, death in a belief, or actual death.

The commands on the maps inside lead to an endless cycle with no resolution. They are locked in a bind in a closed box.

- The daughter is diagnosed as having cancer. Her map states that she goes to her mother whenever she is sick. Her mother's map states that she is a healer with natural medicines. The daughter gets sicker; the mother tries harder to heal. Despite warnings from family and friends the daughter will not see a doctor after the first diagnosis. She dies in her mother's arms at home.

- Christy told me a story of her friend who got a new dog and put it on a leash and went to bed. During the night the dog pulled at the leash to the point it strangled itself. The dog only had one direction, forward, no reverse in its map of what to do at the end of a leash.

- Long ago when calculators first came around, I had contact with an American company making them. This is what happened in a nutshell. The company leadership's map demanded that their company's product was the best little calculator around. Despite warnings from declining sales and foreign inroads into his market, the calculator, its price, and their approach never changed. This continued for a few years until finally bankruptcy was the only solution.

- She gave him an ultimatum, "Quit drinking or I'll leave!" He kept his old map with the bottle, and she made a new map and left. He is now alone.

A Time for a Change

Change begins the minute an openness exists for outside inter-vention. The unresolvable bind has become so unbearable and unacceptable that relief is more important than their maps. The pain of the powerlessness from following invalid maps supersedes keeping them, even with so much of their fears and personality invested. The *Change Navigator* can now directly intervene with the following three actions:

1. **Raise the possibility of a solution outside their world with questions.** Have you considered the possibility of another solution? Is there another way of seeing this problem? How long have you been doing this? Aren't you getting tired? What if there is another way? What if there is an easier way to do what you're doing? What if you are wrong, then what? If you had the ideal, what would it be? Why do you insist on doing things the hard way? How much is it worth to you to stay in this situation? How much is it worth to you to get out?

   What makes their situation unresolvable is not seeing any other way than the one their map dictates. They can't see a resolution, or they would of have tried it. These questions are used by the navigator to raise in their minds the possibility of an outside alternative. Don't give them any more. Timing is important. They may need to stew for a while and think about solutions they have never considered.

2. **Teach them about mindset maps.** What they may need is another language, one outside their experience. Changing the language used may change perception. Doing this may help them separate their maps from themselves. Get it out in front where you can talk about it without being a threat. This book makes this one point.

3. **Show them their problem map.** Another simple thing a navigator can do is to clarify and define what their bind is. They may have never clearly seen what it is bothering them. Often no one has taken the time to help them see what their problem is. I have seen many times when just defining the problem works miracles. People for the first time can see exactly what has been bothering them.

   Write down something in front of them. You be their hand. What they tell you is written down in front of them. Make a map of their map. Use their words and write and erase with only their input, until they accept it as being mostly accurate. I've never had a problem doing this. They usually are very appreciative.

Transcendence to a New World

The only way out of an unresolvable bind is transcendence—a new map in a new box. This unresolvable bind is at the center of most of our problems and the key element leading to growth. If we didn't have binds, we wouldn't change. Only by having a problem without a solution do we ever look beyond our world (box).

When help to solve the bind is requested from the *Change Navigator*, the remapping process begins. The bind in the box creates a de-mand for resolution, the questions and clarification create the possibility of a solution, and the navigator offers the alternative.

133

Second Stage
Remapping

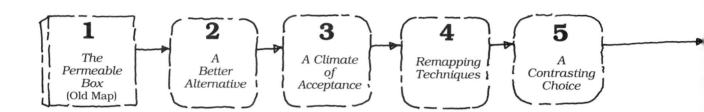

*Often the biggest agent for helping the **Change Navigator** offer an alternative map is change itself.*

This second stage is much easier but more sophisticated in its approach than the last stage. This stage of the remapping process for changing another's mindset maps has five steps:

1. A Permeable Box

This step occurs when the following things happen:

- An individual's or organization's mindset map doesn't accurately represent changing circumstances anymore.
- They are willing to listen to a *Change Navigator* with an alternative. They may have an open mind, but is it open to you?
- They haven't invested their personality into their problem map's continuance or are willing to divest from their map and face their fear of losing it.

The main indicator of this step is when the question "Is there another way I'm not aware of to get me where I want to go, and can you (The Navigator) show me what it is?" is being asked. This one question opens things up for a navigator holding a better alternative map. It can be asked in many ways, some not even verbally, but it must always be there for the remapping to begin. The choice to adopt a new map is always theirs.

A navigator can help others traverse the distance between their old world and their new world. A navigator assists in a transformation.

A word of warning: Don't fall for the ruse of a fake question indicating openness to remapping. I have fallen for it too many times; please learn from my stupidity. Beware of fake openness from a map which wants to create only the image of an open person, not the reality. I have found a map box with hardened walls masquerading as one that is permeable to be one of the biggest conflicts navigators have. Don't get caught in the entrapments and collusion of a superior, or fear-filled map, all the while thinking it is a workable permeable map. To illustrate this pseudo change:

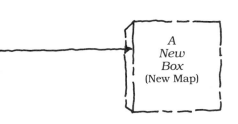

- I was once involved in an educational program with both state and local school systems at the elementary level. Its purpose was to improve learning. All the right things were said about change, improvement, concern for helping kids, and a good deal of effort and money were invested. But when the kids took jumps in learning and grade levels beyond what the system could adjust to, and certain people got the jobs in the system they wanted, the whole thing was quietly shelved. Underneath was the real map of self-aggrandizement, and when it was threatened, the status quo must be maintained. The whole thing was a sham; any real improvement causing real changes was not tolerated. I could have avoided all this if I had followed a consistent indicator for this kind of masquerade with all the words being using to hold up the image of change—an image-management program, not a reality. Too much talk of change is just that—talk. The intention of all the change rhetoric is usually its opposite.

The Remapping Process is a process that is difficult to teach in a noninteractive setting such as this book.

- Here is the story of an extremely competent friend, Sharon. She had requested a meeting with her division head to talk about needed changes. The climate in the office had been deteriorating ever since the rumor had been circulated that top management was reorganizing her department. At the beginning of the meeting Sharon's manager expressed these words, with seemingly heart felt emotion: "I'm very open and willing to work on changing the department for the better and would greatly appreciate your important help and input in doing this." A fellow employee, who had barely kept her job during a previous reorganization, warned her about this man. It seems he turns into a Mr. Hyde from a Dr. Jekyll during times of corporate change, and cleverly uses people's words to discredit them. But sincerity was an art to this guy, and Sharon wanted to believe his words. She went on for hours outlining in detail what she would do. After the session, he shook her hand in warm appreciation and said, "Your ideas and strategies are a Godsend and I will start using them immediately." Sharon took his words to mean the opposite of what actually happened. This manager proceeded to bend the intention of all she had said to him and involved the people she had mentioned in a public flogging—her own. She became the reason for all the department's problems. Under a blaring barrage of change rhetoric and one sacrificial lamb (Sharon), everything was restored to business-as-usual.

2. A Better Alternative

The next step is up to the navigators. They must have something better. Years ago the federal government had a brilliant idea to help the Hopi Indians. It would have helped them live better, with modern conveniences like indoor plumbing and electricity. But the Indians wouldn't accept it. What was the matter with them? The idea was to sell their land and move them all into mobile homes in Los Angeles. Our society is touted as being superior to their stable community that has existed for over 800 years, while ours sometimes looks like it is up to its neck in quicksand yelling for lead hats. Change only for change's sake in a rapidly moving world is foolhardy. If you as a navigator don't have or can't find anything better than what is already there, then for another's sake, retire until you do.

3. A Climate of Acceptance:

Without a setting of trust and willingness to accept what the navigator has to offer, everything is like pushing sleeping and constipated pregnant elephants uphill—a great deal of effort with little gained. I have found one way this climate is created is by a history of consistent performance with a willingness to accept another's destination even while using your maps.

My son was in his teenage years and we were having problems with him (your condolences accepted). As with most teenagers the world centers on them and only their needs. Seeing the larger picture of another person or the whole family is not their strong point. It seemed he was taking more and more until we hadn't much left to give. But he had a problem. Things weren't working out as he wished. Friends, expectations and his own worth were having problems. Then I hit on an idea. I sat down with him and I simply asked him what he wanted and needed and I stayed with it until he agreed that I understood it. Some of his problems were that he just didn't know how to get what he wanted. We established a higher judge than either one of us—the truth. Comments of, "You don't understand me," were now put aside for awhile.

We usually had just bunted heads in confrontations but did something I had never done until that day. I accepted it as all right to have his needs and his wants. But we both agreed they weren't being met the way he expected. So together we proceeded to work out some alternative approaches to get his needs met. I was on his side. His entire manner changed towards me from that day on. A year later, I knew something very significant had changed between us when he told his friends he thought I was his best friend.

A perfectly normal oscillation between accepting the new map and going back to the old one often occurs.

A place of safety free from judgement can also help create this climate. Going from one map to a new map is like a trapeze artist flying from one swinging bar to the next. You first have to let go of the one you are holding and fly through the air before you can grab hold of the next bar. It is being in the air without anything to hold onto that causes this fear. A lifetime of validation in a map that may have once been very successful is a hard thing to leave. This fear can be excruciating. Having a stable and sane navigator can be enormously comforting. They may need to become dependent on the navigator until they can get their feet wet and sail into the new territory on their own.

4. Remapping Techniques:

A person with a map in conflict with reality can't readily see any outside alternative. Anything not in his or her world or map's box is very difficult to conceptualize. People cannot easily comprehend something that lies outside their frame of reference. They may feel something is off more than know why it is. Their feelings, which are holistic impressions, give overall impressions which can be very accurate in indicating something is wrong with the old map, but they typically lack the clarity and direction in providing a specific new map solution. These people with obsolete maps may be ready,

Definitions in the dictionary are comparisons of one thing to another. All knowledge may be essentially metaphorical in nature.

willing and able, but without a conceptual link to the new map, they are blind to seeing any alternative even if it's right in front of them. This is where a navigator, familiar with the new map, can be of immense help. The following techniques can be used singly or in combination when creating this link between the old map and the new one.

A. Provide a metaphorical link between the new map and the old map. A metaphorical link is using something in substitution or in comparison with something else to suggest a commonality between the two. An organization that is called a dinosaur indicates an inability to adapt, thus becoming extinct; an employee who is considered a team player communicates that the individual will follow the group; and a sales technique is compared with fishing to teach the importance of using the right bait. A metaphorical link is based on the idea that within the center of a new map that the navigator is proposing is a concept that is contained within some part of the old map's world. Within the essence of the alternative is an abstract generalization that also exists somewhere within the person's experience and knowledge. If this common framework or conceptual core between the two map's worlds can be found, a navigator can get the person to comprehend the alternative he or she is proposing and its validity. Here are some examples:

- This book is a metaphorical link, hopefully connecting my experience with yours. The commonality between our two worlds is through the simple metaphor of a map.

- The discovery of the function of the heart had to wait until the technical invention of the pump. The inability to see the heart as a pump was due to the fact that mechanical pumps weren't a significant part of the cultural scene until the sixteenth century. When the metaphor existed, the conceptual connection could be made by William Harvey.

- Years ago I worked on an interesting project. It was to find a better way to teach foreign students American history. At the university it was a required course, and these students always had problems with it. They consistently found our history useless and irrelevant.

  The methodology that finally worked was metaphorical. Central ideas in American history were abstracted or generalized and linked to numerous other contexts within the student's lives. For example, an economic concept causing the Civil War was first taught, then linked to biology, then to chemistry, to business and finally to their own culture. The success of this was phenomenal. We even had foreign students teaching Americans their own history. Many of these foreign students said, "This is the best class I've had here. I've learned more in it than in any other."[15]

- Dede was having problems with her church. She had spent years wrapping up her self-definition in providing service to others within its structure. The church's leadership was demanding of her obedience to rules and instructions they never followed. Seeing this discrepancy made things even worse, until I gave her a simple metaphor of an organization being a vehicle for self-interest. Dede saw what they were doing to her in the name of Christ and left to create her own life.

In times of approaching storm, the distant calm belongs only to those who have prepared.

137

B. Give a new interpretation to the evidence supporting the old map. All confirmation and validation of maps is built on or supported through inferred proof. The situations around a map are interpreted as supporting the map. The old invalid map was originally built on and/or maintained through the interpretation of evidence. To illustrate:

• I must be in New York City because there is the Statue of Liberty, the Empire State Building and King Kong.

• I must be a victim because Geraldine tried to destroy my proposal that would have saved the company, with her slanderous statements, behind-the-scene manipulations and counterproposal.

If a navigator can go to the evidence supporting the old map, but give it a new interpretation (giving things a different twist) and then link that new evidence to a new map, a remapping may happen. A reinterpretation of the support for past maps can be one of the easiest ways to teach a new map. Examples:

• With Angela we wrote down the ways her mother treated her during all those years she was growing up at home. The fights, the tantrums, the constant bickering. Then she was asked, if this wasn't her mom, what would she think of this person? "This woman is totally crazy!" was her reply. Angela started to see that things there weren't her fault and also that she didn't need to and couldn't fix them. She was just a normal person locked for years in an insane asylum.

• In old, stable markets with products such as toilet paper, shampoo or gasoline, you can't easily increase sales with new consumers. They aren't there. So you take them from your competition.

Toothpaste research always turned up the same data from the customer, with worthy comments on providing good dental hygiene. But someone relooked at the data and asked the question, "If they are so worried about hygiene, how come they brush at such odd times, like before breakfast?" Then a new map surfaced. People really wanted a fresh taste in their mouth from a night of snoring and fresh breath for being close. A toothpaste was created based on this new map and promoted. Sales went through the roof. Customers left their old brands of toothpaste for the new.

• I was working on a multimillion-dollar project for the Pentagon, but things weren't going as expected. It wasn't that things were bad; it was that they were too good. Every stage of development was rapidly accepted with no changes and no corrections. If you have ever worked with the military, you know this is impossible. None the less it kept happening. Then we began to notice things. The project demanded a building. But when the project drawings were shown, the brass only noticed the small office part of the building. It was to be a public building for the benefit of the citizenry, with ideal-sounding slogans pushing all stages of the project's development. Then some of us went back to reread the patterns of what was really going on and things got clear. Millions of dollars of the taxpayers, money were being put into a new building so a division manager could have his office nearer to his home.

Your ability to effectively navigate a new place is only as accurate as the map you are following.

E. Act as if. You can usually get someone to try a test. Just trying out the new map if possible may be all that is needed. Get them to follow the new map and adjust their reaction and viewpoint to its parameter, if only for a limited time. With the experience of the new map they will they have the conceptual base to understand the map and see its benefit. Keep the venture out of their world safe and easy to return to the old box and show how easy it is to get back. Have them see how little is lost, if anything, and how much can be gained, presumably a lot. If their world can be kept safe, most people will try a little test of acting as if the new map was right. For example:

- An automobile designer from Ford told me the story of when Ford's sales where declining. All their cars looked like variations of a shoe box. Top management tried something different after their design director said he didn't blame the customer for not buying a Ford. He wouldn't buy one of their cars either. Irked, an insightful management then asked this design director to come up with the kind of car he would buy and gave him the go-ahead and resources to make it. Everything was dictated by the design director; even engineering had to follow his instructions. What happened was a breakthrough—the Taurus, one of the most popular cars in automotive history.

- In a design drawing class I watched as students would labor for hours over their drawings, some spending over 40 hours on a single drawing. If that was done in a professional setting, a business would be losing money. So I tried something. I got them to do a drawing in 40 minutes, not 40 hours. I pressured, nagged, pleaded and forced them into doing a specified drawing before they walked out of class that day. It worked. They did it, and the rapid drawings were better than those they had labored on for hours. All the wasted time ended; they couldn't go back to their old way.

- Wesley didn't like his boss, but he liked his job. He wanted his boss to leave so he could stay. He said the boss was just like an overgrown child in need of attention. He expected him to act different and be more adultlike, I guess, and he wasn't doing it. So when things got so bad he couldn't talk of anything else, I exasperatedly said, "If he acts like a kid who needs attention, then treat him like one and give it to him, and let's get on with things." Something way back in the dark recesses of Wesley 's mind snapped and he did a dramatic turnaround. He tried reacting to the boss differently, and his boss responded differently. Wesley even went so far as to put up an ad by his desk with little kids playing on it to remind him how to treat his boss.

F. Reveal the hidden maps that were unknown. The conflicting problems with the old map may be that its owner is unaware of maps being used and games being played right under his or her nose. Bringing these maps into awareness may be all it takes to dramatically change someone. The maps you bring to the surface may be those of others or even their own maps. They may be following maps that they have never clearly seen, and drawing these maps out right in front of them on a sheet or board can sometimes be an enlightening experience. This map awareness gives a person more and faster control over the remapping process. The invisible is now seen. But check to make sure one factor is always present: they want to and can face the exposure of these hidden maps. A few examples:

- This charity donation fund was the top one in the state. It professed the most help to the most people in need of help. Things went fine until it was exposed by the media what luxury the fund's director lived in.

- John couldn't understand why his fellow supervisor acted so strange and mean towards him at times, but at other times acted fine, even friendly. John thought he had some disease or illness that acted up occasionally, causing the strange, mean behavior. This had been going on in various ways for over 15 years. One day, just after one of these reaction times from the other supervisor, he asked me what I thought. (It is nice to have others think you are so brilliant. Hope they don't find out the reality. I wasn't hampered by the situation and could see things in other ways than in the pre-established ways.) The answer was obvious after simply watching the other supervisor in action, but to make sure, I had John describe other similar situations with the similar reaction by this person. I was right and the pattern clear. This supervisor always went bonkers against John any time he received any reward or recognition for his work. Showing John this pattern made years of odd behavior suddenly consistent, and John, now aware, could protect himself against it in the future.

To succeed with this approach, you must have the power of their obedience in order to overcome the commands of their map with commands of your own—like these:

• Do the absurd opposite extreme of what they are doing.
• Do the same thing they're doing, but according to a set schedule.
• Do what they are doing, but much better.

My two boys were arguing until I commanded that they always do it louder, calling each other worse names. When their laughter started, the arguments ended.

- When I was a kid, I had some friends come over to play poker with me at a cabin the family owned. They were eager, too eager. I should have guessed something was up. We played for the next few hours and they took all my money. But then they blew it, when they kept snickering. I found out what was going on. The were playing with marked cards. "Funny joke, but give me back my money!" I suppose if it were the old West, I should have shot them, but being friends and all. . . A year later they even tried it again. But once aware, I was not fooled again.

F. Demand specific new actions in order to reset the commands dictated from the old map. Old maps can be blindly followed as guides into a seemingly endless cycle of the same reactions to the same interpretations of the same events. It is as if these people thus caught are on autopilot and can do nothing else but be a robot, obedient to the commands of the old map. If a navigator has the ability to convince these people thus locked in this endless cycle to follow the navigator's commands over the commands of their old map, a new map can be reset. A high amount of surprise, trust, intimidation or fear of the navigator may be necessary for this kind of obedience, Those thus caught in an old map, but wanting to get out must dance a different dance, sing a new song and play another game. Some examples:

- During one of the many nineteenth-century riots in Paris the commander of an army detachment received orders to clear a city square by firing at the *canaille* (rabble). He commanded his soldiers to take up firing positions, their rifles leveled at the crowd, and as a ghastly silence descended, he drew his sword and shouted at the top of his lungs, "*Mesdames, m'sieurs,* I have orders to fire at the *canaille*. But as I see a great number of honest, respectable citizens before me, I request that they leave so that I can safely shoot the *canaille*." The square was empty in a few minutes.[4]

• Another argument was developing between my wife and me, but for some strange reason some part of me told me not to react the same way. I didn't do my usual when arguing. She was talking to me, voicing her concerns, and I stayed quiet. As I sat on the bed listening to her, welts appeared on my arms! I actually saw them rise. I have never had this happen to me before or since. Then that same part of me whispered something. I suddenly realized that I was at war with my dear wife and didn't know it. I would set her up for argument and win every time, and that war was taking its toll.

When showing them their map:

1. Work out the wording of their old map until they agree with it.
2. Then show the unresolvable bind until they agree with its wording.
3. And finally show the alternative map with its conflict-resolving characteristics.

5. A Contrasting Choice

Pretend you are a fish, like a carp (stay with me now), and your world is all water. You are full of water, your food is full of water, water is above, beside and below you. Everything is water. Then how would you discover water? Wait a minute, how would you discover something that is everywhere? The answer most people come up with is that you would have to get out of the water. The way to discover water is by understanding the absence of it or seeing a contrasting alternative. Remember the old painting in beginner science texts with the bell jar containing a dead bird, surrounded by a scientist, a woman and a little girl crying over the dead bird. It is used to show you how they discovered air (oxygen). It was by creating a vacuum. Unless we have contrast, we can't see anything. Without black there is no white. Without pain there is no pleasure. Without up there is no down and so on . . . We often forget this obvious fact of contrast.

1 Their Old Map

2 Their Unresolvable Bind

3 A New Map

I've had incredible success with just one simple technique of putting the old map next to the new map on a single large board in front of people, showing the old map and the new map in juxtaposition. I especially like those white boards that use felt pens with built-in copy machines. You can leave everyone with contrasting maps that they built. But just a large sheet of newsprint will do. This is how I do it:

1. I first take from them their old map, always the one they want to give, and I put it in their words. Any corrections are theirs, and I proceed until I have the map to their satisfaction. I have never had a problem doing this.

2. Then I put in the seemingly unresolvable problems they may be having with their map, again working on refining it until they agree that I've about got it. Don't even attempt to make it perfect, and tell them so.

141

If all involved don't accept the approximation of what you are doing, you could be there until you fossilize.

3. Next, I draw out an alternative map, with their permission, with statements from me saying, "What if . . . and could it possibly be . . . or consider this for a moment . . ."

During all this I'm always trying to keep things safe by putting supporting evidence around both contrasting maps. I avoid directly contradicting their old map. Both these maps must be in a single viewing. They must see everything laid out before them (I use a lot of abbreviations). Their focus must be on their map and its alternative and not on me or anything else. This makes these visualized maps the center of everyone's attention.

I've even done this with people with very conflicting maps. With a few ground rules, such as letting me draw it all out before they contradict, and respecting differing viewpoints, things have gone very well. Simply seeing things together and in contrast can often initiate a switch to a new map.

New Map for a New World

The essence of what a *Change Navigator* does is to provide alternatives. Navigators do this by presenting or helping to find a new map reflecting a more accurate description of the existing reality than the previous map. Navigators create these alternatives through their skill of discernment in reading things as they really are and their skill in showing others what they have read. When they have success and their alternatives are adopted, growth, success and adaptability may happen. But this is a continuous process of changing and updating maps. Once a new map is adopted, even if very successful, change always continues and the process starts over again. Here is an example from a town and from my own family and how both views of the world were made open to change through new maps:

Park City, Utah, was a silver boomtown located in the mountains behind Salt Lake City, but the silver ran out in the early 50s. The community faced extinction. What was a mining town to do when there was nothing to mine? With outside help the town leaders rethought and saw new resources with mountains, powder snow and an international airport an hour away. They made their town into a ski resort and a recreation center boomtown of the 60s.

But after a number of years the skiing slowed down and the town changed again and it needed to see itself anew. It became a bedroom community to the nearby large city with a freeway connection. It didn't die; it adapted to the changes and became a boomtown again in the 70s with housing.

Now, the town is facing another challenge. The town is rapidly becoming the kind of place that people used to move away from. Park City is losing its sense of community and becoming clogged with cars and streets and buildings. In the past, every new solution to the town's survival came from a redefinition of what the town previously was—their map changed and changed again. The future became an opportunity. The question is now, can the same town adapt again?

A Personal Example of Dramatic Change

My wife and I had a perfectly healthy 18 month-old-boy named Joshua. Then a family member who was also a doctor noticed Joshua's pale gray coloring. He had become sick. We thought he just had a case of the flu. But in minutes my wife found herself riding with Joshua in an ambulance to the hospital. Time proved crucial. He would have died if it was any later without medical help. We found out later our son had spinal meningitis.

My wife called me at work from the hospital. I quickly drove over to be beside her and Josh. A rapid change was happening in all of our lives. Each of the next few days felt like it would never come to an end. We spent most of the time not talking much, just staring at a little baby who was more tubes and wires than child, waiting for any sign, or a word from anywhere or anyone, to hang some hope on.

He came back from the edge. His recovery was as rapid as his decline. We were elated. Joshua was alive and hungry, but our joy was soon squashed. A quiet settled over our previously noisy child. Out of the doctor's mouth came these words, "Your child is deaf." The disease and the efforts to defend against it had destroyed his hearing. His cries became muted. His world became silent. We didn't know what to do or how to react. Crying didn't help; words of encouragement from friends and family didn't help. Wishing things were different didn't help. The feelings we felt were of being hopeless, drowned in a sea we never chose to swim in.

The expectations of a normal life for Josh, just like our other kids, were dashed. Now having a handicapped child who was once perfectly normal seemed too much to bear. We fought the whole idea of his deafness, hoping for a miracle that never came. For a long time we just couldn't accept the reality of everything changing in just one week. The expectations of a typical life with a conventional family doing only the usual things were gone. No matter what my wife and I did, we couldn't stretch our minds to accept what was happening to us. Events were out of our control. I even gave up listening to music for a long time because every time I heard the music I loved, I thought of Josh and that he wouldn't hear it.

Watching him struggle for acceptance and to be understood even

143

when he was so little was very painful. But events wore us down, and we had to come up with a new way of viewing our child and ourselves. We had to completely redo our maps of what Josh would need to grow up. This change in our lives demanded it. It was not a desirable place to be, but we were in it regardless. The question surfaced, did we want to be in it with some power or just swept along with the current?

Understanding the idea of maps gave us some power. It made an unpleasant situation more tolerable. The biggest problem with deaf children, we soon found out, is with learning language. The natural mechanism for learning to communicate had been damaged. This inadequacy of language could affect him both socially and mentally. We all use words to be a part of society and to do a large part of our thinking and conceptualizing. Deafness had thrown us into the totally new world of deaf education. Josh had to be taught language. Josh had to go to deaf school as soon as possible. A little mind is very fluid at first and is ripe for learning the entire framework for language, but as time progresses it sets up and is never as open as before. His mother had a very hard time seeing her little child of almost three go out the door to school when other kids his age should be at home.

It proved very helpful to read the maps of the people involved in our son's deaf education. For example, with one teacher assigned to teach Josh, we read on her map that she thought deaf kids were retarded. We had Josh transferred to another teacher who was herself partially deaf, and her map definitely said she was not retarded and deaf children were very special. Josh did very well under her instruction.

We read the maps of our friends and family. People would often tend to ignore or avoid Joshua, not out of meanness, but from reading their maps, it was just fear. We confronted their fears and put them at ease. Josh was accepted. And his shy smile helped a lot in this area.

We also knew our child needed the help of the organizations created to help the deaf. So we read the maps of the people in power within those organizations. This proved extremely helpful. With a certain administrator we kept our distance. We read that he was using the kids and a part of the deaf program to advance himself personally. He did this under high-sounding statements and his "special program." We saved a good deal of precious time by avoiding sending Josh into this masquerade.

Josh is doing fine. The problems of deafness are often there, but other things have compensated and even excelled to help him. He has developed artistic and mechanical skills that would leave you stunned at his level of ability at such a young age. I have an art background and I remember the others kids calling me into the living room to show me what Josh could do. I stood there watching with my mouth open as I saw him draw with a speed and accuracy I had never seen anyone do before. Communication is still a problem, but he is doing much better. He has a base in language that works well. This new world didn't prove to be as bad as we had once thought.

Always Wanting to Only Redecorate the Same Old Mental House

To help ourselves and our son more, I only wish in looking back that we had used map reading more and stopped all the absurd fighting we did at the inevitability of this dramatic change in our lives. I wish we had made the most of what was really happening to us, seeing things the way they were and not pretending it should be different. But the ideas in this book were only at their beginning stages. Change is hard and it often hurts, but it is a fact in all our lives.

The typical reaction to most changes is just to move the furniture around or add on to a room, but keeping the same old mental house you have been thinking with for years—even when the changes happening will take moving to a whole new neighborhood. It is done this way because it has usually worked in the past and often worked very well. But we are facing a new kind of change where the previous approaches won't work, and if we don't face it in totally new ways we may face some form of death in our lives, like with the continued survival of a town and a little boy.

I believe we can only survive the drastic nature of the kind of changes we are increasingly facing and the ones this book is talking about through a change in our perception. The changes now appearing with increasing regularity will take a whole new mindset. Our old mental house is inadequate, and we can't make do with some easy expansion or adjustment to it. And to quote, Abraham Lincoln, **"The dogmas of the past are inadequate for the stormy present and future. As our circumstances are new, we must think anew and act anew."**

Graduation

From Change-Navigator School

Well, it is time for the final exam, to get your wings, sails, compass, or whatever a *Change Navigator* gets and become an official member of the top secret organization for navigators that everyone is talking about. But before all this, you've got to take the exam. Don't be nervous; here it is:

Check any of the multiple choices that are applicable to each question.

1. Do you have a situation needing change in any of the following situations? ❑working ❑sleeping ❑interacting with family ❑relating with friends ❑choosing your clothes ❑attending school ❑going on vacation ❑attending church ❑television watching ❑jogging ❑partying ❑conversations ❑anything else

2. Is the future going to change? ❑yes ❑maybe ❑drastically ❑occasionally ❑just a little bit ❑I dunno

3. Who is buried in Grant's tomb? ❑Tom Thumb ❑Count Dracula ❑Ulysses Simpson Grant

Grade your own exam. I trust you. Count the total number of checks made. Divide that number by the number of letters in your mother's maiden name, times by pi, and subtract your birthday. Now if you have a final number, well done! It's an "A" grade. You're on to to graduation.

Cap and gown rental is optional. Make a nice graduation certificate with some crayons. It is now commencement and in my usual long-winded manner I'll give the commencement speech:

I was teaching a drawing class, and after working on the same project for too long, I decided to take a break and wander down the hall. I happened into another drawing class. The teacher had left and the students were gathered into a large circle still working on each of their drawings. Whatever they were drawing had left the center of the circle. It was empty. Each student was working in very different media such as felt pen or water color, charcoal, oils and was drawing in his or her own unique style.

If I wanted to know what it was that they were drawing, I could have looked over just one student's shoulder and caught some idea. But instead, I walked around and looked at each student's drawing, making heavy breathing sounds mimicking their teacher (this made them nervous, thinking it was their teacher, until they turned and saw who it was). Collectively, I had a better idea of not only what they were all drawing, but who and what had happened. By looking at each student's artwork, I created a complete image in my mind's eye of what went on and who was involved even though they were

147

not there anymore. Collectively I constructed a total image of an empty center from seeing all the separate viewpoints. Also, I knew they had had a party from the food stains on the paper, and I know who their teacher was from his style of corrections over their drawings. I could even interpret from those corrections that he was having a very bad day.

There are many things that may be hidden, obscure, or lost which can only be understood through experiencing many different contexts. A single view isn't enough to get the whole picture. As with the drawing class and finding out what went on by walking around and seeing various points of view, many other things can be seen and understood only from multiple viewpoints. There is a different type of learning that only comes this way.

Something is going on that I feel will radically change our shared future, and I get it from multiple viewpoints. A few Indian friends, changes in the weather, futurists, some crazy artists, an occasional odd economists, etc., collectively show me something in the invisible center. Our future is about to change as never before. We are all about to witness some very dramatic changes in our world. Take care, navigator, the journey in the next years is going to prove itself to be very interesting and eventful. Prepare to adapt. Prepare for a journey into unknown and exciting waters.

We all sit around in a circle and suppose,
While the secret sits in the center and knows.

Robert Frost

Please hum the usual graduation music, *Pomp and Circumstance*, and hand the graduation certificate to yourself. Congratulations, you're now an official *Change Navigator*. Welcome to *The Benevolent Order of Change Navigators*. Remember their sacred motto: "The map is not the territory."

See you later,

KURT

Sources

1. Omni Magazine Judith Hooper *May, 86*

2. Gaining Control Robert F. Bennett with Kurt Hanks and Gerreld Pulsipher *Franklin Institute, Inc.*

This book has a good decision-making model in it that can support the remapping process. Pocket Books reprinted it if you want it cheaper.

3. The Structure of Scientific Revolutions Thomas Kuhn *University of Chicago Press*

A classic which first clearly presented the concept of a paradigm. Talks about paradigms in the scientific world, how they function and change.

4. Change Principles of Problem Formation and Problem Resolution Paul Watzlawick, John H. Weakland, Richard Fisch *W. W. Norton & Company*

The best approach to change I've found in a therapeutic setting. Takes what a few top therapists, who had consistent, incredible results, were doing to cause rapid change and puts it down into a unified approach. Very similar to what others and I are discovering about dealing with change. Must be some natural laws about change here someplace.

5. The Power of Silence *Carlos Castaneda Simon & Shuster*

I believe this is the best and clearest one of a series of books on breaking our conventional perceptions. It is a look into a totally different culture. The concept of self-reflection and the need to control fear and stalking your self-importance are interesting and helpful from this book's unique vantage point.

6. The March of Folly from Troy to Vietnam *Barbara Tuchman Alfred A. Knopf*

A brilliant work taking historical examples from the Trojan Wars to the Vietnam War on how leadership continues in a mode of reacting to change detrimental to their own self-interest because they are following old maps.

7. The Road Less Traveled *A New Psychology of Love, Traditional Values, and Spiritual Growth* M. Scott Peck, M.D. *Simon & Schuster*

The factors and stages of change are very consistent in this classic on spiritual transformation. There are some very unexpected and unconventional results from actively dealing with changing maps. I found that this book touches on some of them.

8. The Continuum Concept *Jean Liedloff Alfred A. Knopf, Inc.*

The only cultural example I could find that doesn't have the rigid validating boxes endemic to our society. It contains a possibility on how to rid ourselves of the problems caused when people confuse their maps with themselves.

9. The Tao of Leadership *John Heider Humanics Limited*

Great summary of the Chinese Book of Change (or how change happens) for dealing with contemporary organizational situations.

10. Grow or Die the Unifying Principle of Transformation *George Lock Land Random House*

The entire book centers on one natural law pushing everything towards growth through three separate stages. He applies this law in an incredible number of varied contexts.

The following books are part of the Quick Read Series:

11. Getting Your Message Across
12. Up Your Productivity
13. Wake Up Your Creative Genius
14. Motivating People *All by Kurt Hanks and Crisp Publications*

15. Relational Learning Handbook *Kurt Hanks Unpublished Manuscript*